Practice and Feedback for Deeper Learning

26 evidence-based and easy-to-apply tactics
that promote deeper learning and application

Patti Shank, PhD

Deep Learning Series

Copyright © 2017 by Patti Shank PhD/Learning Peaks LLC.
All rights reserved
v2.2017

All rights reserved. No part of this publication may be reproduced, distributed, or transmitted in any form or by any means, including photocopying, recording, or other electronic or mechanical methods, without the prior written permission of the owner, except in the case of brief quotations embodied in critical reviews and certain other noncommercial uses allowed by copyright law.

For permission requests, email patti@pattishank.com.

License: The purchaser of this book has an **individual license,** which means the purchaser bought a single copy. The author also sells versions for expanded distribution, which are marked with a group or site license.

Quantity discounts:
This book is available in print and electronic formats on Amazon and from pattishank.com. To obtain quantity discounts for your work team, class, or workshop, contact Patti: patti@pattishank.com.

Patti Shank PhD/Learning Peaks LLC
Learning sPeaks Publications
www.pattishank.com

Practice and Feedback for Deeper Learning/ Patti Shank PhD—1st ed.
ISBN-13: 978-1976215087
ISBN-10: 1976215080

Praise for *Practice and Feedback for Deeper Learning*

Patti's book is absolutely brilliant. It covers most (if not all!) fundamentals for effective learning design. It also reminded me that our profession is tough! There are many nuances and subtleties that are extremely important. Patti explains these complicated topics in an understandable and applicable way.
Mirjam Neelen, MSc., Learning Experience Design Lead

Patti Shank's *Practice and Feedback for Deeper Learning* should be on the bookshelf, physical or virtual, of everyone who creates instruction for improving the performance capability of their target audiences. If you are concerned with transfer back to the job you will benefit greatly from following her five strategies and 26 tactics. This is now the second book I would have every L&D staffer read after Mager and Pipe's *Analyzing Performance Problems*.
Guy W. Wallace, President, The Enterprise Process Performance Improvement Consultancy

The training industry is full of myths and misconceptions. Even experienced professionals with the best of intentions can spread these myths and misconceptions to their fellow professionals. Organizations depend on good training to enable employees, at all levels, to succeed and deliver real business value. But myths, misconceptions, and just plain misinformation can fail your learners, your organization, and yourself. How do you overcome this? Read Patti's book. Read it cover to cover. Revisit it often. It is an inoculation against the worst training abuses, and a prescriptive remedy for driving your training efforts toward a healthy situation. But don't just read one book. She is writing a series. Read them all. If you are not a trainer, demand, ask, beg, borrow, or bribe your training professionals in your organization to read and apply what she shares. She has done the work of collecting the best and brightest, and her books are now in that pantheon of best and brightest on their own.
Bill Sawyer, Director, Global Learning Services, Seal Software

Most of us don't have time to read dozens of research articles to learn the best strategies. Fortunately, Patti Shank has done the hard work for us, sifting through the research and summarizing the key strategies and tactics in a way that's easy to understand and apply. *Practice and Feedback for Deeper Learning* tackles two critical aspects of learning: Practicing skills and providing feedback to improve learning. This book explains tactics you can use immediately to create memorable, relevant practice activities and to provide feedback that helps learners get more out of those practice activities.

Christy Tucker, CIDD, Syniad Learning

Acknowledgments

A recurrent theme in my work is people who make my work and me better. If you see good work, I have help. (If you see problems, they're likely my own.) I am extremely grateful and they inspire me to look for ways to help others.

Special thanks to Amy Sitze. I truly doubt I'd be doing any of this work without her early coaching.

Thanks to Bill Sawyer and Mirjam Neelen for reviewing the book in advance and helping me make it better. I am very grateful.

This work uses tools that are expensive and hard to obtain. Without my personal superheroes Brent and Jessica, I couldn't do it.

Table of Contents

Introduction 1
   Why Are Practice and Feedback Needed? 2
   How This Book Works 3
   Using This Book 4

The Science 7
   Deep Learning 9
   Learnability 11
   Prior Knowledge 13
   Memory 14
   Mental Effort (Cognitive Load) 18
   Social Processes 20
   Transfer 25
   Metacognition 29
   In Your Own Words 32

Why Practice and Feedback? 35
   Why Are Practice and Feedback Important? 35
   Practice 41
   Feedback 44
   Five Strategies and 26 Tactics 47

Strategy 1: Analyze the Job Context 49
   Tactic 1: Connect Learning Objectives to Job Tasks 50
   Tactic 2: Analyze Conditions Under Which People Perform the Tasks 54
   Tactic 3: Evaluate What Must Be Remembered and What Can Be Looked Up 57

    Tactic 4: Analyze Social Processes 62

    Tactic 5: Find the Typical Misconceptions 64

    Tactic 6: Find Out What Gets in the Way 66

    Tactic 7: Assess Support for Skills 70

Strategy 2: Practice for Self-direction 73

    Tactic 8: Work Toward Specific, Difficult, and Attainable Goals 74

    Tactic 9: Use Self-directed Learning Strategies 77

Strategy 3: Practice for Transfer 83

    Tactic 10: Make Training Relevant 84

    Tactic 11: Build Practice that Mirrors Work 89

    Tactic 12: Show the Right and Wrong Ways 99

    Tactic 13: Train How to Handle Errors 101

    Tactic 14: Use Whole-skill Practice 102

    Tactic 15: Help with Post-training Support 107

Strategy 4: Practice for Remembering 111

    Tactic 16: Use Real Context(s) 112

    Tactic 17: Use Self-explanations 118

    Tactic 18: Space Learning and Remembering 120

    Tactic 19: Support Memory with Memory Aids 126

    Tactic 20: Support Essential Skill Upkeep 132

Strategy 5: Give Effective Feedback 137

    Tactic 21: Keep the Focus on Learning 138

    Tactic 22: Tie Feedback to the Learning Objectives 140

    Tactic 23: Offer the Right Level of Information 144

    Tactic 24: Fix Misconceptions 148

    Tactic 25: Give Feedback at the Right Time 154

Tactic 26: Structure Feedback for Ease of Use.................160
Now What? 163
   Retrieval Practice 165
   Practice and Feedback for Deeper Learning Checklist......... 173
   Want More? 179
   References 181
Index 195
Notes 199
About the Author 203

CHAPTER 1

Introduction

This book is significantly different from many other books about using the learning sciences to make learning better in that I have put a lot of effort into finding out what *training* research says, rather than what general learning research says. If you develop training or learning for adults or professionals in the workplace who must gain or maintain skills, this difference may be important to you.

Most books that discuss adult learning research use research from higher education (sometimes even K-12 research). Higher education research may or may not be directly applicable to training settings since the goals and purposes of training are vastly different from those for higher education. Training participants themselves have many differences from higher education course participants. The organizations that offer training have different goals from universities and other higher education institutions.

As a result, when I started writing this series, one of my goals was to find the researchers and the research in training and applied adult learning settings (like professional development). I'm delighted that training has a robust research base from which we can make recommendations for *training* and more applied adult learning practices.

In the rest of this chapter, I will tell you why I started writing these books and offer some ideas on how to use this book to improve your skills.

Why Are Practice and Feedback *Needed*?

Without certain types of practice and feedback, we don't get better at what we do. If you've ever wanted to learn a new skill and muddled through the steps with a few other participants—and then went back to your work—you may still muddle through the steps or forget how to do it at all. You may understand the "why" of the skill but not really know the "how." And even doing something over and over doesn't mean you are improving. (Practice doesn't make perfect. Perfect practice makes perfect.)

There are words I repeatedly misspell as I write. I notice this as my word processor repeatedly corrects the exact same words. And, because the tool does it for me, I don't improve. Recently, I stopped to see which words autocorrect continually corrects and I noticed that I always misspell *sentence*. However, because I noticed this, now I can spell it correctly.

Research tells us that, when people attend training, not that much makes it back to work. There are many reasons for this (and I'll talk more about it in Chapter 2) but a large part of the reason is that people do not get enough—or the right kinds of—practice and feedback. A training "event" is typically not enough to change knowledge and skills long term. As Helmuth von Moltke the Elder said, "No battle plan ever survives contact with the enemy." In other words, when your plans and the real world meet, the real world wins. This is most certainly true with training.

The work people do often cannot be reduced to simple step-by-step tasks, as is too often attempted in training. People work in complex and often stressful environments for which we often don't account in training environments. Often, we don't offer realistic-enough opportunities to improve skills. As a result, people simply continue to do what they know to do—even if organizations would benefit greatly from improvements in skills.

Truly meaningful practice and feedback are often absent from training. Training should be less about content development and more about people development. We shouldn't start by analyzing what we need to teach. We should start by analyzing *what people need to be able to do*. What people already know and what people need to be able to do will come up repeatedly in this book. They are key practice and feedback issues.

The learning sciences are complicated, but the good news is that applying them isn't nearly as complicated. The intention of this series is to offer information about what the learning sciences say and, more importantly, how to apply that information.

Research shows that work increasingly involves complex mental tasks and frequent updating of skills. This reality has huge implications for practice and feedback, which is why this is the second book in the Make It Learnable series. The Make It Learnable series applies key learning, writing, and information design principles to remove obstacles to learning and help people learn, apply, and remember needed information.

The ability to help people learn, apply, and remember is one of the critical keys to supporting today's work challenges. We need all kinds of people to teach others in this world. The more capable and skilled people there are in the world, the better the world is for everyone. I discuss building training, but you should be able to apply it to other adult learning settings as well.

How This Book Works

After this brief introduction, I offer an overview of the science (research) that supports the five strategies and 26 tactics described in the book. I write in mostly non-academic language (but I use some academic terms to help you understand why we need the strategies and tactics in the rest of the book).

I then discuss key research-focused strategies and tactics you should use to make your instruction better meet today's learning conditions in organizations. My goal is to help you create valuable instruction that builds needed skills.

Using This Book

This book presents five specific strategies. For each strategy, I discuss actionable tactics you can implement this very moment. For each tactic, I show examples and discuss issues. Here are the five strategies I will discuss.

Strategy 1: Analyze the Job Context

Strategy 2: Practice for Self-direction

Strategy 3: Practice for Transfer

Strategy 4: Practice for Remembering

Strategy 5: Give Effective Feedback

How to improve *your* skills using this book

Throughout this book, I suggest ways to practice the skills listed. But don't wait for me! There are two excellent ways to strengthen your understanding, and I suggest doing both.

- **Summarize** each section in your own words. Research shows that "self-explanations" are a powerful method for increasing understanding. This simply means summarizing in your own words, which helps build a model of the topic in your mind (in academic terms, this is called *building schemas*). Use this instructional method in your courses, too!
- **Apply** each section to your own content. If you know of others who are using this book, share how you apply the tactics. Offer feedback to each other.

When should you use these strategies and tactics?

This book applies specifically to adult learning in organizational settings. It applies generally to professional development and other applied adult learning settings. If you need the people you are teaching to learn specific skills and use them on the job or elsewhere in life, this book offers specific ways to make your instruction more relevant, applicable, and memorable.

In the next chapter, "The Science," I begin by discussing the learning science that supports the strategies and tactics discussed in the rest of the book. Understanding the science helps you understand the choice of strategies and tactics in the rest of the book. For example, why is it so difficult to transfer skills from instruction to the workplace? Why do we need to worry about not overloading people while they are learning?

I love this content because research shows it makes a real difference in learning outcomes. If you have suggestions for improving it, I want to hear from you. I am self-publishing the Make It Learnable series, so I can easily maintain and update it. You can get in touch with me through the contact form on my website (www.pattishank.com) if you have comments to make it better.

Before you move on...

Strategy 2 in this book is *Practice for Self-direction*. In that chapter, I describe how self-direction helps people identify their own learning needs; set learning goals; identify resources, materials, and tools; plan and implement learning activities; and evaluate their outcomes. There are specific aspects of self-direction that research shows can improve learning outcomes.

To improve *your* learning outcomes from this book, consider using a few of these strategies before we move on.

- Skim the book table of contents and index. What are the *most important* knowledge and skills *you* hope to gain from the book?

- Why are the knowledge and skills you named important to you?

- What kinds of practice do you think you will need to gain the knowledge and skills?

CHAPTER 2

The Science

This part of the book explores core research ideas that help us understand how the right kinds of practice and feedback help people gain and maintain needed skills. It explains the whys behind the how-tos in Chapters 4 through 8. Knowing why helps you understand the how-tos.

Some of the content in this chapter is very close to the content of Chapter 2 in *Write and Organize Deeper Learning*. I added sections on deep learning (which is the purpose of practice and feedback) and transfer of training (which is part of the secret sauce of deep learning). I added new examples and explanations in response to questions readers asked. Restudying materials (spaced learning and spaced practice, which I discuss in Strategy 4), helps you remember this information. Reading it again helps you more deeply learn.

Practice is performing a behavior or task for perfecting the outcomes and, in many cases, being able to remember what to do without needing support. Research on the differences between novices and experts shows that people with more expertise learn differently and, in many cases, more easily. If you want to perfect your skills (at electrical wiring, writing reports, making cakes, planning parties, or anything else), the ability to add new skills more easily can be its own reward. People who want to get good at something often create their own deep learning so they can get where they want to go. They may read books, select goals to reach, practice to reach those goals and then set new ones, find people with more skills to coach them and offer feedback, and more. This is the essence of deliberate practice, which is needed to gain skills past the average level. Anders Ericsson, an important researcher on the science of expertise, explains extensively what deliberate practice is and how people use deliberate practice to become expert.

There are seven areas of research that give us insight into practice and feedback needs for deep learning (Figure 2.1).

Figure 2.1 Areas of science that help us develop deep learning through practice and feedback

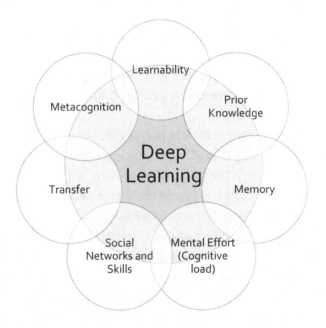

Insights and outcomes from these research areas help us understand how to make learning work better for people in today's fast-changing work environments. The examples in the following sections come primarily from adult learning and learning in organizations. If you work in other areas of learning, I highly recommend you make specific connections to your areas of learning and instruction.

Deep Learning

Until the 1970s, the issue of "depth" of learning wasn't discussed or researched. Two professors at the University of Gothenburg—Ference Marton and Roger Säljö—did groundbreaking research on the depth of mental (cognitive) processing while learning, which began a continuing conversation about (and research into) what they called surface and deep learning approaches and their outcomes.

Marton and Säljö asked students to read an article and then answer questions about it. They transcribed the conversations and analyzed them, finding two different approaches to reading and interpreting the article: surface and deep. A surface approach focused on the main points. A deep approach looked for the meaning behind these points and how they related to each other and other knowledge. Other researchers have since studied surface and deep approaches to learning and have found critical implications for learning outcomes.

Figure 2.2 shows progress from surface learning to deep learning on a continuum.

Figure 2.2 Continuum from surface to deep learning

Surface → Deep

The following Table 2.1 shows the primary differences between surface and deeper learning approaches (available in references). For example, I started out as an optician after graduating from university. When training opticians, learning the *refracting* (light bending) power of lenses in plus (+) or minus (−) *diopters* (refractive power) may start with a shallower approach—as first steps to understanding physics related to bending light (optics).

Table 2.1 Differences between surface and deep learning approaches

	Reason for learning	**Learning tasks**
Surface	Learn for short-term use, as for course requirements or testing	Enough effort to meet requirements Accept concepts at face value Remember content, if needed
Deep	Learn for long-term use, as for application	Effortful understanding Relate content to already-known information Find underlying patterns and principles Apply learning to personally important problems Critically examine logic Come to conclusions

At first, soon-to-be opticians learn these physics concepts and terminology, such as refraction and diopters, without knowing how to use them. Without going further, those concepts don't have much context, so it is hard to remember them—and difficult to use them. But soon they learn the properties of different lens materials. They use these concepts and terms to verify prescription lenses using a lensometer.

Surface learning is not *bad*. But it is usually not enough for applied skills. Deeper learning is needed to gain and maintain usable skills. This book concentrates on deep learning approaches using relevant and meaningful learning tasks and strategies. You don't have to know what those are just yet. I'll explain them simply and with a lot of examples.

The following are two of the most important implications of deep learning for instruction.
- ✓ We need to help people learn deeply—both in formal instruction and on their own—as jobs are becoming less routine and more complex.
- ✓ Deep learning approaches support application and usable skills.

Using the tactics in this book will improve how your instruction supports skill building. This is one of the most important things *anyone* who creates or facilitates learning and performance can do.

How would you explain deep learning in your own words? How does deep learning apply to the instruction you build? Go to page 32 and explain learnability and how it applies to the instruction you build. Don't skip this! It will help you understand and remember this concept!

Learnability

Learnability is the ease and speed with which something can be learned, applied, and remembered. Learnability applied to learning in organizations means people can easily use instruction, performance support, and other tools to get work done and improve skills (complete tasks, fix problems, and so on).

In *Write and Organize for Deeper Learning*, I discussed how two concepts help us understand learnability: readability and usability. Readability is the ease with which a text can be read and understood. I showed how to compute readability statistics and how to think through readability for your audience(s).

Write and Organize for Deeper Learning concerned itself mainly with how to make instructional content easy to understand and use. That's a foundational skill for building good instructional content. If people cannot easily understand content, not much else matters.

We often assume people will be able to understand what we write because *we* understand it. That isn't the case. I wrote this book using Microsoft Word and checked the readability using Flesch Reading Ease. It scored 53.9, which means the writing is at about a ninth-grade reading level.

Good usability for learning and performance means building them with real-world use in mind. We will discuss this in several places in the book, starting with Tactic 1: Connect Learning Objectives to Job Tasks. And designing for learnability also means creating content that helps people gain and maintain skills. This requires learning at a deep level. Otherwise, we are wasting resources and not doing what we can to help people gain and maintain needed job skills for today's workplace.

Learnability is important to deep learning because anything that is easier to understand and use makes deep learning easier.

The following are two of the most important implications of learnability for instruction.
- ✓ Learnability requires designing for good readability and ease of use.
- ✓ Making instruction and performance support materials optimally usable helps people perform better and build and maintain skills.

How would you explain learnability in your own words? How does learnability apply to the instruction you build? Go to page 32 and explain learnability and how it applies to the instruction you build. Don't skip this! It will help you understand and remember this concept!

Prior Knowledge

What people already know forms the foundation for understanding and remembering new information. When we learn, new information alters what we already know.

To make sense of new information, we mix new information with prior knowledge. And, as we learn more information, our schemas (how information is organized in long-term memory) are updated (Figure 2.3). The more complete and accurate our schemas are, the easier it is to use them to solve problems and deal with a variety of situations. More complete and accurate schemas allow us to act flexibly in a variety of situations.

Figure 2.3 Unorganized bits of information (left) and organized schema (right)

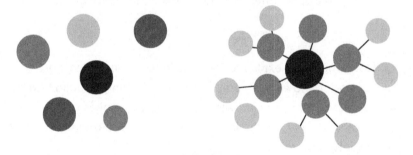

When people have no schema for knowledge and skills they are learning, they depend on us—the expert, trainer, instructor, or instructional designer—to help them build schemas, even though they won't say, "Can you help me build complete and accurate schemas?" What they say instead is that they don't understand. Or can't see how things relate to each other. Or they say nothing because they are confused.

Building accurate schemas is one of the primary outcomes of deep learning. Practice and feedback are critical for building them. Accurate schemas help us do our work, solve problems, and continue to learn, which is one of the most important reasons for using deep learning approaches.

Connecting what people know (prior knowledge) to what they are learning is one of the best tools for helping people understand.

The following are some of the most important implications of prior knowledge for instruction. We
- ✓ Cannot assume people have a certain amount of prior knowledge.
- ✓ Cannot assume people understand the information we present. We need to figure out if they do.
- ✓ Need to connect what we are teaching to what people already know. This helps added information stick.
- ✓ Must find and fix misconceptions. Building new knowledge on a faulty foundation leads to even more misconceptions.

How would you explain prior knowledge in your own words? How does prior knowledge apply to the instruction you build? Go to page 32 and explain prior knowledge and how it applies to the instruction you build. Don't skip this! It will help you understand and remember this concept!

Memory

John Sweller, a well-known educational psychologist and researcher, explains that *human cognitive architecture* (how our mind and memory works) has constraints we should take into consideration when building learning and performance materials. Figure 2.4 shows the basic memory processes happening during learning.

Figure 2.4 Learning processes and memory

Environment: Sensory inputs (sights, sounds, feelings, etc.)

⬇

Senses: Take in environmental information.

⬇

Working memory (WM): Compare new information to prior knowledge; filtering irrelevant information.

⬇

Long-term memory (LTM): Store and retrieve memories.

Our senses take in information from our environment. Working memory (WM) uses prior knowledge to 1) filter out information we don't think we need and 2) select essential elements for processing. This filtering occurs because of the large amount of environmental input, but WM can handle only a small amount of new information at a time. WM has limited capacity (the amount it can process) and limited time (how long it can hold it).

If information is retained in long-term memory (LTM), it alters prior knowledge by adding to it—and is transformed by prior knowledge by giving new information meaning. To understand memory and its impact on learning, it is helpful for us to understand two specific memory processes: encoding and retrieval.

Encoding

To move information from WM to LTM, information is stored. This process is called *encoding*. We can remember the word "encoding" as memory **codes** in our mind, as in Figure 2.5.

Figure 2.5 Encoding is storing information in LTM in specific formats (codes)

There are three main ways we encode information:
- Visually, as images
- Auditorily, as sounds
- Semantically, as meaning

When you say something over and over to remember it (like a phone number or someone's name), you are trying to encode it auditorily. Most encoding is semantic (meaning), which has a lot of implications for remembering (retrieval).

Encoding semantically means we store information along with the context (situation, emotions, location, etc.). Therefore, one of the strategies we can use to help people remember what they learn in training is to teach using the same context as they would encounter on the job.

One implication of deeper learning is to use training tactics that produce better encoding so what is taught is easier to remember.

Retrieval

Remembering is retrieving information from LTM. Because what we store in LTM is more easily retrieved by meaning or association, it's critical we make instruction personally meaningful and relevant to a person's work or life. Research says that, for long-term retrieval, it is best to teach in the same way people will use the information. For example, if people look up information using a specific tool on the job, they should look up information using that tool during training. We should help people associate concepts that belong together (such as saving, budgeting, and financial well-being) so they are associated in LTM.

When you first start learning yoga, for example, the asanas (poses) the instructor calls out make little sense. Many instructors use the Sanskrit name and, if you are new, you don't know what they mean. Over time—from practicing over and over, from the instructor adjusting how you are doing poses, and from doing the same thing over and over in later classes—long-term memory starts to form associations. If the instructor says to soften your knees, you know what it means. And you can then do the sun salutation series at home because you do them in class each time and have learned the progression of poses.

Encoding and retrieval are key elements when learning. As a result, this book offers tactics for deeper encoding and easier retrieval. If we don't design with memory constraints in mind, far less learning occurs and transfer from learning to on-the-job application is less likely.

The following are a few of the most important implications of memory for instruction.
- ✓ WM is a limited resource. We must take its constraints into account when creating learning and performance materials.
- ✓ We need to design with as few unnecessary demands on WM as possible so people can deal with the demands of learning (no extra content or distractions).
- ✓ We should design for optimal encoding and retrieval.

In a very real sense, learning equals the potential for changing what we know and can do. Designing for encoding and retrieval is critical for deep learning as it helps us apply what we are learning.

Question: Does encoding happen during training?
Answer: Encoding is a process. It can begin during training but people can easily forget what they don't regularly retrieve and use. So we should also provide memory assistance and retrieval practice, which can make essential information easier to remember and retrieve.

Go to page 32 and explain memory and how it applies to the instruction you build. Don't skip this! It will help you understand and remember this concept!

Mental Effort (Cognitive Load)

When we understand that working memory (WM) needs to process all new information but has considerable constraints (in capacity for new material and holding time), we realize WM is one of the most important constraints we must deal with when designing instruction. (Accurate and adequate prior knowledge, on the other hand, *helps* people learn.)

A person I once worked with told me her training group had to train on large quantities of information very quickly. "It's like drinking out of a firehose," she said, and she asked how they could do it better. My response was a bit too abrupt, but it's true nonetheless: Anyone who must drink out of a firehose will die of thirst, because you cannot drink out of a firehose.

Sweller reminds us that design must be *with* how memory works; otherwise, people can't learn. His research shows that cognitive load is the amount of mental effort needed to process current information. Working memory—the part of memory used to process information in the present moment—can deal with only so much content at a time. Too much information overloads working memory.

We learn most effectively by comparing knowledge in working memory to knowledge in long-term memory (prior knowledge). A working memory clogged by attempting to handle too much content cannot do this. Our ability to make sense of what we hear is impaired with too much noise. Our ability to learn is impaired with too much to learn at once.

Not all cognitive load is the same. Some is helpful; some is harmful. **Harmful cognitive load** is mental effort that wastes effort to learn, remember, and apply. Some examples include:
- Extra content that isn't on target or that isn't needed now
- Non-valuable or decorative graphics
- Unnecessary explanations
- Images in a different place than their explanation
- Media that doesn't allow stopping, starting, and rewinding

Helpful cognitive load is mental effort that helps people learn, remember, and apply. The following are some examples.
- Self-check exercises
- Analyzing wrong answers
- Putting what you read into your own words
- Practicing tasks until they are easy to do

This is a good time to clarify that not all good cognitive load is fun. "Necessary to learning" and "fun" are two different things. Part of learning—especially when learning harder things—is making it through the hard parts until they become easier. You know this if you've learned to play an instrument. Or a sport. Can you think of other things you have struggled to learn?

Robert Bjork, Professor of Psychology at the University of California—and a well-known researcher and writer on memory and learning—has written extensively on the topic of "desirable difficulties." His research and writing say that the right kinds of effort are critical to being able to apply what we learn. You will see his work reflected in some of the tactics in this book, such as explaining the key terms in your own words. This may seem like useless work, but self-explanations (putting concepts in your own words) are very desirable difficulties. It helps you understand and remember. Desirable difficulties are especially important for deep learning.

The following are two of the most important implications of cognitive load for instruction.
- ✓ Build instruction that supports helpful cognitive load and eliminates as much harmful cognitive load as possible.
- ✓ Use desirable difficulties that help people remember and apply.

We must make sure we are not overloading memory while learning.

How would you explain cognitive load in your own words? How does cognitive load apply to the instruction you build? Go to page 32 and explain cognitive load and how it applies to the instruction you build. Don't skip this! It will help you understand and remember this concept!

Social Processes

When people talk about learning, they often mean how *each person* learns, remembers, and applies what he or she learns. It's true that, when we develop instruction, we must consider how our strategies impact individual learning. But it's also true that, in organizations and elsewhere, work is completed not only by individuals but by groups of people. Teams, departments, and other groups of people—and even larger groups of multiple teams, departments, and organizations—are needed to get work done.

For example, when I write a book and do the research and writing, there are others who make the process possible. I work with an editor or two. I use online information to learn how to self-publish. The things others do impact what I know and can do.

Albert Bandura, an influential psychologist who is well known for his views and research on social learning, researched how we learn from each another. The primary ways are by observing their behavior and the outcomes of their behaviors.

Obviously, we see what others say and do. We receive others' work products and they receive ours. There are important social components that affect our work and work outcomes. Most work is part of processes that are affected by coworkers, leaders, vendors, or customers. With the increase in globalization, companies and people are socially connected across borders and other traditional boundaries.

Rapid changes to demographics, technology, and organizations are causing more need to work (well) with others. Knowledge work—work that uses analysis, evaluation, and creation tasks for knowledge products such as reports, training, briefings, diagnoses, and so forth—requires good social skills. Researchers say that jobs affected by technology now rely on social skills more than ever before. Jobs are quickly changing and skills for any given job are becoming less stable. This means skill needs change—and learning quickly and on an ongoing basis is the new normal.

Social skills are hard to automate. Jobs continue to morph. The world changes rapidly. And people need to work together to complete their increasingly challenging work. Dr. David Deming, Professor of Public Policy, Education, and Economics at Harvard, describes how social skills at work are becoming just as important as cognitive skills for higher-wage positions. Social skills minimize the costs of coordination between people, teams, and companies, which allows people to efficiently work together. We can look at news headlines to see the damaging effect of poor social skills on companies and the people who work for them.

Table 2.2 shows common social channels for learning both inside and outside of work. For example, when we collaborate with others, everyone working together can learn through the successes and mistakes of all. During on-the-job training, more experienced people can learn better ways to help others learn and may be able to see things through the eyes of their trainees. Social learning can and often does go in more than one direction.

Table 2.2 Social learning channels in the workplace

Channel	Description	Who learns?
1. Work	Watching work, learning from work and collaboration	Everyone involved can learn from work and lessons learned
2. Questions	Learning from gaps in knowledge, questions, and answers	Everyone can learn from each other's answers
3. On-the-job training	Formal and informal on-the-job training	New people learn from more experienced people, but learning can go both ways
4. Helping linkages	Formal and informal mentoring and coaching offer insights and connections	New people learn from more experienced people, but learning can go both ways
5. Formal training	Centralized or decentralized classes and programs help people learn knowledge and skills	New people learn from more experienced people, but learning can go both ways
6. Social media	People can connect with others to get help and find connections	New people learn from more experienced people but learning can go both ways

Social learning contributes to deep learning by offering many channels for learning and ways to contribute.

Interactivity

Research reflects a lively debate over the definition of interaction and interactivity. Ellen Wagner, a well-known analyst and researcher in our field, contends that interaction occurs when "objects and events mutually influence one another." Although some differentiate between interactions and interactivity, I believe Wagner's definition makes sense for personal and technology interactions and the resulting interactivity.

Michael Moore, Professor Emeritus in the Department of Learning and Performance Systems at Pennsylvania State, wrote an often-cited paper on types of interaction and the need for interaction during learning. Although he was writing specifically about distance learning, these interactions hold true for blended and face-to-face learning as well. Table 2.3 describes the three types and lists some examples of each type.

Table 2.3 Three types of interactions

Type of interaction	Description	Examples
learner-learner	Interactions between participants	discussions small group activities virtual classroom chat
learner-instructor	Interactions between participant and the instructor	questions help resources
learner-content	Individuals interacting with content	text multimedia

How interactivity supports learning

Interactions support learning in diverse ways. Terry Anderson—Professor Emeritus at the Centre for Distance Education, Athabasca University—discusses four ways learning interactions support learning (notes in parentheses are my own).

- Learner control (which can lower cognitive load)
- Participation (which can improve engagement and interest)
- Meaning making (which can contribute to deeper learning)
- Alternate perspectives (which can contribute to deeper learning)

Because interactions are so critical to learning, Anderson developed an "equivalency theorem" stating that deep learning can still occur if one or two of the types of interaction are at low levels—or may even be eliminated if the remaining is truly optimized.

To decide which interactions are *most* critical, he explains that learner-instructor interactivity generally has the highest perceived value. But some instructor interactions may be automated (for example, automatic response emails) and built as learner-content interactions (for example, expert answers).

When job tasks require social skills and collaboration, job-related social interactions in training should not be left out. In other words, learner-learner interactions that mirror realistic social interactions must be a critical part of training. Tactic 11 discusses practice for these interactions.

This is critical: Interactions should foster deep thinking and learning. Learning activities that do not further this goal may only add pointless mental effort (cognitive load).

Interactions should help people learn deeply and apply learning.

Transfer

I said earlier that we need to design for deep learning because deep learning helps people apply their skills. Training transfer means people can apply, to their jobs, the knowledge and skills learned in training. Training transfer is a critical outcome, yet research in training and learning shows that transfer doesn't happen easily.

Research says transfer from instruction to the workplace is problematic. We must design for transfer. Fortunately, there is a lot of research on transfer of training—and we can use that research to help us design more transferable training.

Lisa Burke, Professor of Management at the University of Tennessee–Chattanooga, and Holly Hutchins, Associate Professor of Human Resource Development at the University of Houston, performed an updated training transfer literature review (analysis of academic sources on a specific topic). Their review tells us the likely factors that most influence transfer. Table 2.1 lists major factors they found to influence transfer.

For each major factor, I added what Timothy Baldwin, Professor of Business Leadership at Indiana University, and Kevin Ford, Graduate Director of Organizational Psychology at Michigan State University, found to most influence training transfer.

Training without transfer is training that isn't applied.

Table 2.4. Factors that affect transfer of training, adapted from Burke, L.A., & Hutchins, H.M. (2007). Training transfer: An integrative literature review. Human Resource Development Review, 6, (3), 263-296.

Major factors that impact transfer	Major influences in each factor
Work environment	Work climate
	Opportunity to use trained skills
	Supervisor support
	Peer support
Design and delivery	Learning goals
	Content relevance
	Practice and feedback
	Behavior modeling
	Error examples
	Cognitive load during training
Personal characteristics	Mental ability
	Self-efficacy
	Anxiety
	Openness
	Perceived utility
	Job involvement
	Organizational commitment

Strategy 3 discusses specific tactics that affect transfer.

Work environment

Research shows that the work environment greatly influences whether training transfers. Burke and Hutchins found that the four work environment influencers listed in Table 2.1—what they call "transfer climate"—make transfer likely. For example, when supervisors and peers support the skills learned in training, transfer is more likely. If they don't, it's harder to perform as trained, even if people want to perform as they were trained.

Research finds specific supervisor behaviors to be helpful, including participating in training, discussing the training with staff, and encouraging people to use newly trained skills. Peer support for using newly trained skills also helps people transfer training to the job. But, when supervisor support is lacking, peers have less influence than if the supervisor supports the training. People also need opportunities to use newly trained skills. Not having that opportunity is one of the largest impediments to transfer and it makes remembering what was learned much harder.

Because work environment factors can make or break transfer, we should figure out if there will be a positive climate for the newly trained skills before we spend time building instruction or other support materials.

Design and delivery

Burke and Hutchins' findings also say which design and delivery variables are likely to make transfer more likely. For example, they found that clear learning objectives help inform participants what they are expected to do and which aspects of performance are important. Clear learning objectives are found to help participants focus their attention and put in needed efforts. I discussed writing clear and job-focused objectives in *Write and Organize for Deeper Learning*.

Content that is relevant (to the job) improves transfer. People want a direct relationship between training tasks and work tasks. And certain training methods also correlate with more transfer. We'll discuss those methods in Strategy 3. Since helping people learn complex skills can create cognitive load, we need to remove as much harmful cognitive load as possible. I discuss cognitive load in this chapter and there are writing and organizing techniques that impact cognitive load in *Write and Organize for Deeper Learning*.

Personal characteristics

Personal characteristics also impact transfer. Burke and Hutchins' findings say mental ability influences transfer because greater mental ability translates into greater ability to focus and maintain attention. A person's thoughts about their capacity to learn what is being taught also impact transfer. But a person's thoughts about their ability can be improved. Strategy 2 discusses tactics to help participants feel more in control.

The degree to which people value their career and the degree to which they are committed to organizational goals influence transfer. These feelings are part of what is called *engagement*. There are other factors that contribute to engagement as well.

The following are a few of the most important implications of transfer for instruction.
- ✓ Transfer is one of the most important reasons for training.
- ✓ We must design for transfer.
- ✓ We need to evaluate the transfer climate. If it is low, transfer is far less likely.

Designing for transfer is one of our most important responsibilities.

How would you explain transfer of training in your own words? How does transfer of training apply to the instruction you build? Go to page 32 and explain transfer of training and how it applies to the instruction you build. Don't skip this! It will help you understand and remember this concept!

Metacognition

Metacognition is an awareness of one's own thinking and learning processes. (*Cognition* means thinking, so "metacognition" means thinking about your thinking.) It's an important learning and life skill that makes us better and more self-directed learners and workers.

Metacognitive processes allow us to use prior knowledge to plan how to approach a given learning task, monitor our progress, solve problems, evaluate how we are doing, and change our approach as needed. These skills help us apply what we know about ourselves, what we know about different strategies for learning, and what we know about the demands of a specific learning task. John Flavell, an American psychologist, coined the word "metacognition."

It is critical to learn throughout our work life, so, as designers and facilitators of learning, we should embed metacognitive strategies in instruction. Research shows that using metacognitive strategies during instruction helps people learn to apply them elsewhere in their lives.

Plan learning goals

Before instruction, we can help participants
- Look at the content and activities to decide whether they are right for their needs.
- Identify the outcomes that are most important to them.
- Figure out what efforts they need to successfully achieve the desired results.
- Decide what help they will likely need.
- Identify what has worked for them in learning similar things before.
- Figure out what they already know about this task or group of tasks.
- Uncover misconceptions that can mess up their learning.

Monitor progress

During instruction, we can help participants
- Identify what they do and do not understand.
- Summarize the key points in their own words (this helps build schemas).
- Find added resources for areas of interest not covered in instruction.
- Find help.
- Help others.
- Use "help" identified during planning to work on areas of weakness.
- Develop questions.
- Decide what still feels too hard and what they need to do.
- Look for areas of wide confusion (so an instructor or subject-matter expert can adjust instruction).

Evaluate strategies and outcomes

During and after instruction, we can help participants
- Reflect on the learning experience.
- Determine which strategies worked well for them.
- Review initial planning steps and decide whether any changes are needed.
- Develop strategies for learning and applying this content.
- Check in on what is working or not working in their application of the strategies.

Metacognitive strategies are life-long learning skills. We prepare people for the realities of rapidly-changing job skills by using these strategies in our instruction.

The following is an important implication of metacognition for instruction.
- ✓ Use metacognitive strategies in instruction to help people become effective life-long learners.

Using metacognition in learning helps people become self-directed. This is a critical skill as job skills become more unstable.

📋 How would you explain metacognition in your own words? How does metacognition apply to the instruction you build? Go to page 32 and explain metacognition and how it applies to the instruction you build. Don't skip this! It will help you understand and remember this concept!

In Your Own Words

Self-explanations are a powerful tool to help you integrate new and prior knowledge. They involve describing what you learned in your own words.

For each of the concepts in this chapter, explain them in your own words, including how each concept applies to your instructional materials.

Deep Learning

Learnability

Prior Knowledge

Memory (Including Encoding and Retrieval)

Mental Effort (Cognitive Load)

Social Processes

Transfer

Metacognition

CHAPTER 3

Why Practice and Feedback?

Chapter 2 discussed underlying research (the WHY) that helps us understand the need for the tactics in the rest of the book (the HOW). The purpose of the 26 tactics is to build practice and feedback that makes learning deeper.

Why Are Practice and Feedback Important?

The subject of this book is practice *and* feedback. Why did I put these two topics together? It's because they go together like fish and chips, Batman and Robin, peanut butter and bananas (Elvis Presley reference), and snow and snowball fights.

Practice is where we apply what we are learning. It's where people make it meaningful and take it from *what* to *how*. Realistic practice makes learning easier to remember and apply on the job. Think about something you learned and applied to something important to you. What lessons did you learn? (Lessons learned are feedback to yourself.)

Feedback supplies information about needed changes. Figure 3.1 shows feedback (mistakes I circled) from the table of contents (TOC) in Word for a chapter I wrote for someone else's book.

Figure 3.1 Mistakes I circled in my Microsoft® Word table of contents (TOC)

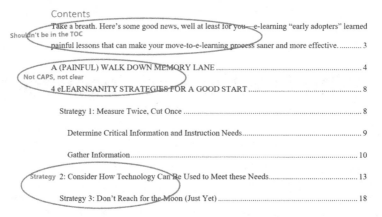

All the things I circled are things I saw that I needed to fix.

Intrinsic versus extrinsic feedback

The feedback from the TOC activity came from seeing what was wrong with the TOC, not from an instructor or another person. Feedback can come from many sources. If we are in a training class, feedback often comes from peers and the facilitator. We consider what others say about our answers and performance extrinsic—or external—feedback. We also get extrinsic feedback when we do an online activity and the screen tells us our answer was incorrect—and why.

Intrinsic—or internal—feedback comes from within or from natural consequences, like burning your hand on a too-hot bowl of soup (or seeing what is wrong with your table of contents). Intrinsic feedback is also real-life feedback you get from a learning scenario that returns the consequences of your choice rather than "learning" feedback" such as "That is an incorrect choice. You should have taken her keys away so she cannot drive while impaired." I show an example of intrinsic versus extrinsic feedback in Figure 3.2.

Figure 3.2 Intrinsic versus extrinsic feedback

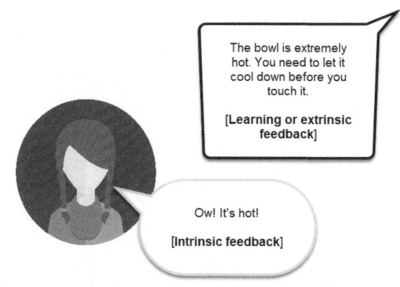

Throughout the practice chapters of the book, I encourage you to use realistic practice methods because they tend to be more easily remembered. This is true for feedback as well.

The relationship of work performance to learning objectives and practice and feedback

How can we decide what instructional practice we should create and what feedback we should use to evaluate it? When learning in organizations, desired work performance directs needed learning objectives. Learning objectives target needed practice and guide evaluation of the practice (feedback). Figure 3.3 shows this relationship visually.

Figure 3.3 The relationship of work performance to learning objectives, practice, and feedback

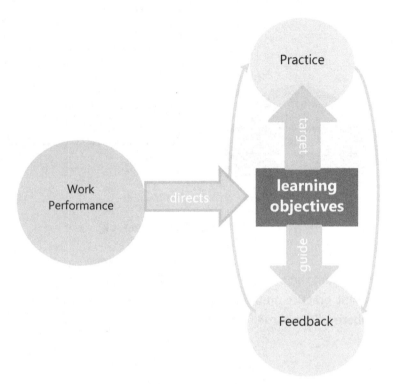

Consider how the process in Figure 3.3 might work with a lesson on using heading styles to build a table of contents (TOC) in Microsoft Word. During analysis, we discover the following document requirements for using a table of contents.

- Use of Microsoft Word Heading Styles
- TOC is after the cover and before the introduction
- No TOCs for documents under five pages
- TOC can have up to three levels of headings (H1, H2, H3) but must have at least one level
- H2 and H3 are used only when there are at least two in a section
- Headings should use parallel construction when it makes sense to do so

- Headings should be understandable to readers
- TOC should not have missing headings
- No non-headings should show up in the TOC
- All headings should show up at the right level

We use these requirements to create the learning objectives. The learning objectives target which practice activities are needed. I show two examples of making practice activities from learning objectives in Table 3.1.

Table 3.1 How learning objectives become practice activities

This learning objective becomes→	This practice activity
Create heading styles using Microsoft Word heading styles	Apply three levels of heading styles using Microsoft Word
Make sure headings are understandable to readers	Review each heading for clarity and make changes as needed

If a learning objective doesn't easily tell you what practice activity is needed, chances are the learning objective doesn't describe specific work performance. I'll discuss this in more detail in Tactic 1. The lesson objectives, practice activities, and feedback checklist might look like Figure 3.4.

Figure 3.4 Practice and feedback for lesson on creating a table of contents using Microsoft Word heading styles

Lesson: **Create Company XYZ-Compliant Document Table of Contents**

Learning objectives:
1. Don't use a TOC when...
2. Create heading styles using Microsoft Word heading styles
3. Use parallel wording in your headings when possible
4. Make sure headings are understandable to readers
5. Add the table of contents to your document after the cover and before the introduction

6. Check for TOC problems:
    a. Missing headings
    b. Headings aren't parallel
    c. Headings not written in reader-friendly language
    d. No more than three levels of headings
    e. When H2 and H3 are used: At least two used in the section?
    f. Non-headings show up in the TOC
    g. Headings at wrong heading level

Practice activities:
1. Apply three levels of heading styles using Microsoft Word
2. Create a TOC in this document (simple)
3. Create a TOC in this document (more complex)
4. Find the errors in and fix the TOC in this document (more complex)
5. Build your own document with TOC (more complex)

Feedback checklist:

Yes/No	All answers should be yes	Issue(s)
	Does the document have more than five pages?	
	Is the TOC after the cover and before the introduction?	
	Are all headings created using Heading styles?	
	Are all needed headings there?	
	Are all headings at the right level?	
	Are headings parallel?	
	Are headings reader-friendly?	
	Are there three or fewer levels of headings	

	Are there at least two headings in a section when H2 and H3 are used?	
	Are all headings in the TOC actual headings?	

Research on practice and feedback says that connecting the right kinds of practice with valuable feedback makes a significant difference in learning outcomes. In the rest of this chapter, I'll discuss what the research tells us about what makes some of the bigger differences in practice and feedback outcomes. Then, in the rest of the book, I'll describe the how-to tactics that put these principles into action.

Practice

Practice is where people apply what they are learning. Jim Williams and Steve Rosenbaum, authors of the book *Learning Paths*, describe a much-too-common problem in training adults in the workplace. The problem is that people are supposedly "trained" but then are less-than-proficient performers. They make costly mistakes and cannot perform at the desired level.

Williams and Rosenbaum say it often takes a very long time for new hires to become independently productive. They define "independently productive" as the point in time when a person can do what they need to do without needing a lot of help or making a lot of mistakes. Getting people to this state, which they call *time to proficiency*, is the most significant contribution training organizations can offer.

I'd add this: Too many training organizations miss this as their primary purpose and do not put into practice what we must do to make this happen. (This is one of the reasons I am writing these books. The learning sciences have so much to offer us in how to improve this situation.)

What Williams and Rosenbaum and many training researchers tell us is the difference between inadequate performers and independently productive performers is the right type and amount of practice.

How much practice do people need? A lot. Here are some of the reasons people need a lot of practice:
- People must connect what we are teaching with what they know. It isn't a simple matter.
- Human memory is slow and gets overloaded quickly. Overloading means little or no learning can happen.
- When bombarded with a lot of information, people forget most of it.
- The training methods that help people learn, remember, and maintain knowledge and skills are not used. We must use them!

Research tells us the right type of practice
- Has specific goals
- Matches the challenge level to current skill level and prior knowledge
- Offers adequate practice to meet the goals
- Supplies the right kinds of feedback

Specific, goal-oriented practice

Training starts with specific and measurable goals. Training goals come not from content but from what people need to be able to do on the job. We know what people need to do on the job from Strategy 1: Analyze the Job Context.

Training that doesn't come from a job context is often just a content dump. And content dumps are poor ways to teach people. Unless we know what people do with that knowledge, we are unlikely to develop deep learning that helps people apply what they learn.

Match practice to current skill level and prior knowledge

Learning is cumulative and builds on what people already know. What we know and can do serve as a foundation or building blocks for learning new things. For example, in this book, I use some examples of training two-factor authentication. A person who has never had to authenticate their identity—such as at a bank, when trying to cash a check, or has never used a computer and passwords—would have a difficult time understanding this concept.

For people with less prior knowledge, we'd train differently and start at a different point. We'd learn what authentication means, why we need to authenticate, how to authenticate your identity, and where you might need to authenticate your identity. Stories could help: Calum's mom had her Social Security payments stolen, and Eva's checks bounced. To start, build practice around some basic ideas: Where might someone expect to be authenticated? The bank? The swimming pool? The grocery store? Work up to practicing two-factor authentication.

Adequate practice

How much practice is adequate? While analyzing the job context (Strategy 1), we need to figure out (usually with stakeholders) the level of skill people leaving training should have (Figure 3.5). How much practice will get people to that level? How will people maintain skills that are rarely used? How will people get adequate practice?

Figure 3.5 Continuum from beginner to expert performer

| Beginner | Can work with help | Independently proficient* | Highly proficient | Expert performer |

* Terminology from Williams and Rosenbaum, *Learning Paths*

We must realize that, if people don't immediately use what they learned, what they learned will start to decay. We must help stakeholders understand what is needed for people to *gain and keep* needed skills.

Feedback

According to John Hattie—a noted educational researcher at the University of Melbourne, Australia—feedback is one of the top ways to improve learning outcomes. But, interestingly, research also finds negative effects! What this means is that people who design and deliver instruction must understand the factors that improve the effectiveness of feedback.

Feedback has several roles to play during instruction, especially related to practice, including:
1. Confirming understanding when understanding is correct
2. Correcting mistakes or misconceptions when understanding is incorrect
3. Closing the gap between what people can do and what they should be able to do (learning objectives)

I will start by discussing the factors that influence the effectiveness of feedback. This information comes largely from Hattie, Valerie Shute (now a professor of education at Florida State University), and Susanne Narciss (professor in the Department of Psychology at Technische Universität Dresde).

Feedback that hurts learning

Research has found that certain types of feedback can result in less effort and reduced learning. They include the following:
- Trivial goals
- Praise
- Rewards

- Comparisons to others, such as rankings
- Threats
- Discouragement

Feedback research finds that praise and rewards hinder intrinsic (internal) motivation; therefore, we should consider not using them. Instructional feedback should emphasize the role of learning and growth in knowledge in skills with time and effort. When people feel unsure or wrong, feedback should help them see how they will get back on track. In other words, feedback should have a support-and-learning focus rather than a performance-at-any-cost focus. Anxiety about needing to perform while learning can make it harder to learn.

 Skill and prior knowledge affect feedback

The amount of skill and prior knowledge a person brings to instruction greatly affect how we should offer feedback. Table 3.2 lists major feedback issues in the left column and shows how we should handle them differently at the different ends of the skill and expertise continuum.

Table 3.2 How skill and prior knowledge of the topic impact feedback

Issues	Lower skill, less expertise in the topic	Higher skill, more expertise in the topic
Type of feedback	More directive	More facilitative
Amount of information	Specific	Deeper understanding
Level	Task specific	Cues, hints, details
Support	More support	Less support
Timing	Immediate	Time for mental processing

One conclusion from Table 3.2 is that we need to understand the types of people we are training. Another is that we need to tailor feedback to the situation. That's why the first strategy in the book is analysis. And Tactic 1 is *Connect Learning Objectives to Job Tasks*. Job tasks are likely to be somewhat (or very) different for people just learning those tasks than for those who are more expert.

Five Strategies and 26 Tactics

Table 3.3 lists the five strategies and 26 tactics discussed in the next five chapters. Consider bookmarking this page as it offers an at-a-glance view of all the strategies and tactics that work together for building practice and feedback for deep learning.

Table 3.3 Practice and feedback strategies and tactics

Chapter 4	**Strategy 1:** Analyze the Job Context	Tactic 1: Connect Learning Objectives to Job Tasks Tactic 2: Analyze Conditions Under Which People Perform the Tasks Tactic 3: Evaluate What Must Be Remembered and What Can Be Looked Up Tactic 4: Analyze Social Processes Tactic 5: Find the Typical Misconceptions Tactic 6: Find Out What Gets in the Way Tactic 7: Assess Support for Skills
Chapter 5	**Strategy 2:** Practice for Self-direction	Tactic 8: Work Toward Specific, Difficult, and Attainable Goals Tactic 9: Use Self-directed Learning Strategies
Chapter 6	**Strategy 3:** Practice for Transfer	Tactic 10: Make Training Relevant Tactic 11: Build Practice that Mirrors Work Tactic 12: Show the Right *and* Wrong Ways Tactic 13: Train How to Handle Errors Tactic 14: Include Whole-skill Practice Tactic 15: Help with Post-training Support
Chapter 7	**Strategy 4:** Practice for Remembering	Tactic 16: Use Real Context(s) Tactic 17: Use Self-explanations Tactic 18: Space Learning and Remembering Tactic 19: Support Memory with Memory Aids Tactic 20: Support Essential Skill Upkeep
Chapter 8	**Strategy 5:** Give Effective Feedback	Tactic 21: Keep the Focus on Learning Tactic 22: Tie Feedback to the Learning Objectives Tactic 23: Offer the Right Level of Information Tactic 24: Fix Misconceptions Tactic 25: Give Feedback at the Right Time Tactic 26: Structure Feedback for Ease of Use

CHAPTER 4

Strategy 1: Analyze the Job Context

Many people who develop instruction start building instruction using the information they have available. Learning practitioners who work in organizations often start with content from a subject-matter expert. They divide the content into logical topics; build slides, handouts, and online pages; and so forth. But starting with the content rather than the job is seriously flawed. We train to develop specific skills, not content. And starting with content often leads to instruction that doesn't focus on the nature of the job and how knowledge and skills are used.

When we don't focus on how knowledge and skills are used, we are asking people to make the leap from the content to how it is relevant to their jobs. But many people—especially those new to the topic—cannot do this. Research on transfer shows that even people who know more have difficulty making this leap. They may be able to pass an end-of-course recall test but are unlikely to be able to apply it on the job. Real engagement is about making content that is *relevant* to the job or life.

Here's what we need to do instead. We need to start with the tasks people do on the job and tie them to what we are teaching. This way, instruction is focused on job or life. It also helps us bound the scope of instruction. If you have read the first book in the Make It Learnable series, *Write and Organize for Deeper Learning,* you may remember that reducing the scope of instruction (to only what is needed and no more) helps with remembering.

Without doing the analysis discussed in this chapter, you won't know how to make your instruction job-centric rather than content- or topic-centric. In Chapter 2, I said the purpose for learning is deep learning, which helps people gain and maintain usable skills. Knowing what people need to be able to DO is the critical first step toward designing for deep learning.

Figure 4.1 lists the tactics I'll discuss in this chapter. When you use these tactics prior to building instruction, you'll know what people need to be able to DO. The other chapters will help you build needed activities and provide feedback to assure participants so they are moving toward the skills they need to have.

Figure 4.1 Tactics that help us analyze the job context

Tactic 1: Connect Learning Objectives to Job Tasks
Tactic 2: Analyze Conditions Under Which People Perform the Tasks
Tactic 3: Evaluate What Must Be Remembered and What Can Be Looked Up
Tactic 4: Analyze Social Processes
Tactic 5: Find the Typical Misconceptions
Tactic 6: Find Out What Gets in the Way
Tactic 7: Assess Support for Skills

Tactic 1: Connect Learning Objectives to Job Tasks

To learn deeply, people need to apply what they learn in their job context. *Our* job is to know how what we want to teach relates to the work participants do. One of the easiest ways to do this is to cross-reference what we are teaching to participant work tasks so we are building instruction that is naturally relevant.

Consider an example. XYZ Safety Training trains workers on various aspects of safety in the workplace. One of their training series is on safety at construction sites. Figure 4.2 shows the learning

PRACTICE AND FEEDBACK FOR DEEPER LEARNING • 51

objectives from their construction worksite ladder safety blended training course. Do the learning objectives seem job-focused or content-focused to you? Job-focused objectives are work skills oriented. Content-focused objectives aren't work skills oriented. They are typically *about*, not *how-to*.

Figure 4.2 Learning objectives for XYZ Safety's ladder safety training course

Learning Objectives

After attending this training and performing the exercises, construction staff will:

1. Name the major risks of ladder falls
2. List the ladder safety steps, in order
3. Differentiate between ladder types
4. List which parts of a ladder need to be inspected

The learning objectives in Figure 4.2 are topic-oriented. Do construction workers name the major risks of ladder falls? List the ladder safety steps, in order? Differentiate between ladder types? List which parts of a ladder need to be inspected? No, they don't. The learning objectives are not job-focused.

Figure 4.3 shows a revised list of learning objectives that are job-focused. Each of the learning objectives is something construction workers do on the job to use ladders safely. Each of them embeds the knowledge construction workers must know to use ladders safely. By building job-focused learning objectives, we are starting the process of building job-focused practice and feedback.

We build objectives before course content because they tell us what people need to be able to do. What people need to be able to do tells us what we need to design to train people to be able to do their jobs.

Figure 4.3 *Revised* learning objectives for ladder safety blended training course

Learning Objectives

To reduce the risk to life and limb from construction falls, you will:

1. Decide which ladder or other apparatus is best to use
2. Inspect the ladder before use
3. Position a ladder safely
4. Use the ladder safely
5. Make a hazardous situation safe

Menu
Click to open

Note that I also changed *construction staff will* to *YOU will* and made the first sentence more compelling. In the first book in this series, *Write and Organize for Deeper Learning*, Tactic 9 is *Talk Directly to Your Reader or Listener*. In that tactic, I discussed how we should write like we are having a conversation with each individual reading or listening. Research tells us that, for learnability, conversational writing is better than formal writing.

Once we have our learning objectives in a job-focused format, we should also make sure the content is job-focused. For example, in Table 4.1. I show the objectives and a very high-level content design for both the initial ladder safety course and the revised ladder safety course. Here's what you should notice. The initial course (on the left) has course content that is topic-focused. The revised course (on the right) is all application- and job-focused.

Table 4.1 Content for initial content-focused objectives (left) and content for revised job-focused objectives (right)

Initial objectives	Content	Revised objectives	Content
• Name ladder fall risks • List ladder safety steps • Differentiate ladder types • List ladder inspection steps	List of ladder risks/Quiz List of safety steps/Quiz Show ladder types/Quiz Show inspection steps/Quiz	• Decide which ladder or tool to use in situation • Inspect ladder before use • Position ladder safely • Use ladder safely • Make hazardous situation safe	Real-life situations: Spot the hazard, fix the hazard Real-life scenarios 1 with job aids Real-life scenarios 2 without job aids On-the-job safety sessions

Question: What if I can't get information about how the content relates to specific job tasks? Someone handed me content and asked me to build a course.

Answer: If you wanted to buy new blinds for your house and the salesperson told you they wouldn't measure your windows but instead would use a generic window size, you'd run! Just as generic window treatments are likely to work poorly for your home, generic training content is likely to work poorly for your participants.

In Tactic 2, we'll discuss additional ways to understand the work context. In Strategies 3 and 4, I'll talk more about why employing the work context is so very important.

Tactic 2: Analyze Conditions Under Which People Perform the Tasks

In Tactic 1, we made sure the learning objectives were specific, work-related tasks. In other words, we described what people should do on the job—NOT what we will teach or the topics. This is because, as you will see throughout the book, there are some central ideas. One of these ideas is mirroring job tasks during practice as much as possible.

One of the most important ways of mirroring job tasks is mirroring the conditions of the job tasks. To understand the job conditions, we must understand the conditions under which people perform the tasks. Figure 4.2 shows a few examples of different conditions for performing a similar task.

Table 4.2 Examples of different conditions for doing the same job task

Task	Condition 1	Condition 2
Share ladders	Handyman	Large construction site
Give medications	Oncology practice	Hospital floor
Update software	Personal computer, update performed by user	Large facility, update performed by IT

How do we understand the conditions?

The reason we want to understand the conditions under which people perform is that it
- Offers clarity about how people can and cannot get work done.
- Helps us understand how different conditions affect training needs.
- Offers insights about real constraints on performance.
- Supplies guidance on useful feedback.

PRACTICE AND FEEDBACK FOR DEEPER LEARNING • 55

To gain an understanding of the conditions that affect the tasks, watch the work and ask questions (best) or simply ask questions. Leaders often do not understand the conditions as well as the workers. Some of the key questions include:

1. What is the work setting like (noise, lighting, temperature, number of people) when you are performing this task? How do these conditions affect your work and the task outcomes?
2. What do you regularly use (tools, information, materials, people) to perform this task? How do the things you use affect your work and task outcomes?

For example, Figure 4.4 shows three screens from three related versions of medication error reduction courses. When developing the instruction, training developers found that medical offices, urgent care, and pharmacies all needed to perform similar tasks to reduce medication errors (double-checking and verification tasks) but, because of the different work environments, different staff, and differences in how things worked in those environments, the processes and training couldn't be the same.

Figure 4.4 Courses tailored to different working environments and staff

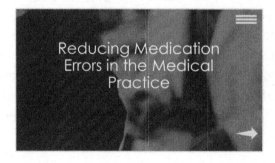

All the conditions?

The conditions in which we are interested are the ones that affect what people do and how they do it. Too many times, training happens as if conditions are always ideal and nothing ever goes wrong. But conditions are often challenging and things *do* go wrong.

Training people well means helping them feel like they can perform well in their typical work conditions and the less-than-typical but likely conditions as well. While I can't tell you how many conditions you should understand, I do know this: The better you understand the realities of the jobs for which you are designing, the better that training is likely to be. I will repeat this frequently.

Tactic 3: Evaluate What Must Be Remembered and What Can Be Looked Up

Knowing how the knowledge and skills we are teaching are used in specific jobs helps us figure out what people need to commit to memory or automate (can do automatically) and what they can look up when needed.

As I discussed in Chapter 2, working memory is a limited commodity that is easily overwhelmed. One reason we must understand job tasks is to understand the need for remembering information and skills so we can use the right instructional approaches during training and on the job.

For example, how do construction workers use the ladder safety skills discussed in Tactic 1? Must they remember these skills or can they look them up when they need to use them? XYZ Safety Training tells us that construction workers may have documents (work orders, supply lists, etc.) with them while working. But they don't know if people would be willing to use job aids on the job. For now, if we build job aids, assume they will be used as memory aids during practice sessions online and during on-the-job practice only (see Figure 4.4).

Because people must remember how to be safe, training sessions and post-training activities will include activities to help people remember. You will see examples of these activities later in the book.

Figure 4.4 Job aid used during the ladder safety course

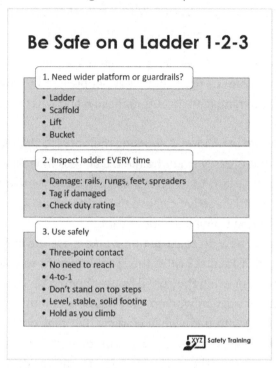

Let's think about other learning situations. What do we need people to memorize and what can they look up? Some people say people can look up everything. But that's absurd.

We cannot know *what* to look up or how to interpret what we look up unless we have adequate foundational knowledge and skills. For example, what if you are having problems connecting to the Internet and the help desk tells you to open the command prompt and use ping to verify network connectivity? For many non-technical people, this would sound like Klingon. I'm sure you can think of many times where you didn't know what to look up because you didn't have adequate knowledge—or had some knowledge but what you looked up didn't make sense to you.

I'm trying to learn beading (jewelry), but many of the books have diagrams and directions I don't understand. What I need is a foundational class that gets me to a place where I can use the information I look up. My husband, an electrical engineer, will sometimes show me diagrams for things he is building. Those diagrams look a lot like the beading diagrams to me.

What I am pointing out is that terminology, how-tos, and concepts mean something to people who are in the know. For those who aren't, they are gobbledygook.

We can look up how to do some things when they need to be done—especially when there is time to do so. For example, a friend bought a house and the toilets didn't work well. So he read about the best toilets online and then bought them at a large hardware store along with the tools and items he needed. Online job aids and videos showed the replacement steps. But, for someone who didn't have some foundational knowledge (how to use the tools, what the terminology meant, etc.), there would need to be additional pre-training; otherwise, even this might be too difficult to attempt.

Figure 4.5 shows a remembering continuum that helps us think through how well people need to be able to remember knowledge or skills (that we are teaching).

Figure 4.5 Remembering continuum

"Remember" and "automate" may sound like the same thing, but "automate" means remembering *without effort*. People need automated skills in life-and-death situations—for example, CPR and advanced life-support skills. There are other skills police, military, medical, and emergency personnel must automate and they regularly practice maintaining automation of these skills.

Remembering means being able to recall from memory. How easy it is to recall falls along the continuum shown in Figure 4.5. Skills used regularly may become almost or completely automated. Skills not used regularly typically decay (decline). Knowing whether skills should be remembered or looked up—and, if remembered, how easily remembered—is part of the job of designing deep instruction.

Figure 4.6 supplies a list of questions that help analyze the need for remembering during *and* after training.

Figure 4.6 Questions to help you analyze the need for remembering

1. Can they look it up on the job?
    a) Do they have time to look it up?
    b) Do they know how and what to look up?
    c) Will they understand what they look up?
    d) Does the information change regularly?
2. Do they need to remember?
    a) Do they have to perform quickly and with accuracy?
    b) Are they expected to know?
    c) Do they need to remember to perform other job tasks?

Answering *yes* to all the number 1 questions likely means people do not need to commit the information or skill to memory. For example, answering customers' questions about the availability of an item falls into the can-look-it-up category. The service rep probably has time to look the information up, will know how and what to look up, and will understand the information they find. That's the job. Question 1d points to a need to look up the information, as the information changes regularly. Item availability may fall into this category.

Answering *yes* to all or most of the number 2 questions likely means people DO need to commit the information or skill to memory. For example, we expect the emergency veterinarian to act quickly and with accuracy when treating a hurt animal. We expect them to know what questions to ask about the injury and what to do with that information.

When you are a novice and just learning, you don't know how to do much of anything. That is the purpose of training. Novice customer service reps get trained and often work with more experienced customer service reps until they reach a certain level of proficiency. Medical residents become more experienced working under attending physicians.

In Chapter 2, I described how prior knowledge impacts learning. We need to think about the knowledge people need to have to benefit from training or performance support. Using the command prompt to ping the network assumes some underlying knowledge and skills:

1. Finding ping using your OS
2. Using ping commands
3. Interpreting ping results

We will see how these issues (remembering, skill decay) become tactics in Strategy 4. In Strategy 2, I will also discuss whose responsibility it is to maintain and upgrade skills, as this is becoming a critical personal and organizational issue as job skills become less static.

Tactic 4: Analyze Social Processes

Individual learning, which is typically the focus of most training and performance solutions, doesn't go far enough. It leaves out a large piece of how we learn.

When I write research reports, I often ask questions to gain others' insights. Those insights regularly affect what I ask and how I frame my work. People who design products often work with potential users before, during, and after the design process. I literally would have nothing to write about if I didn't have others' work to analyze and organize. Whose work do you count on to do your own?

When teaching people how to achieve valuable outcomes, we must include the context of the work, which almost always includes the social learning and social processes in which we get work done.

When working with others, across departments, and across time zones, it's easy to forget that many people need to be working toward the same goals and with each other toward needed outcomes. Helping people learn how to optimize the work of the group (or group of groups) is a massive hole in most training and most performance plans.

Consider the social learning and social skills needs of the tasks for ladder safety on the construction site. Many people might initially think there aren't any social learning or social skill needs. Not so!

Table 4.3 shows a variety of ways we are safe on construction sites and the social skills needed to share resources, use the correct resources, and help others.

Table 4.3 Ladder safety social learning and social processes

Job task	Possible social learning and social processes
Use the right tool	Share limited tools
Safety processes	Ask questions and get advice Hold ladder Get help

Figure 4.7 shows revised learning objectives for the ladder safety training with a new social processes objective.

Figure 4.7 *Revised* learning objectives for ladder safety blended training with social process objective (highlighted)

Learning Objectives

To reduce the risk to life and limb from construction falls, you will:

1. Decide which ladder or other apparatus is best to use
2. Inspect the ladder before use
3. Position a ladder safely
4. Use the ladder safely
5. Make a hazardous situation safe
6. Help others protect their health and safety

Tactic 5: Find the Typical Misconceptions

In Chapter 2, I discussed how prior knowledge affects how new information is interpreted and remembered. Figure 4.8 shows how new information becomes transformed when we connect it with what we already know.

Figure 4.8 Transformation of new information as it connects with prior knowledge

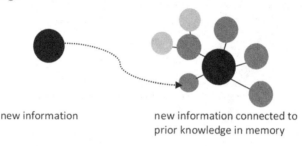

new information　　　　new information connected to prior knowledge in memory

When new information is learned, there are many options for misunderstandings. We can connect new information to the wrong prior knowledge, connect it in inaccurate ways, and so on. And misunderstandings cause difficulties in application and further learning (impediments to deep learning), so we need to make sure people have learned correctly.

We want to do two things related to misunderstandings/misconceptions:

1. **Typical misconceptions:** *Before building training content*, find out what typical misconceptions people have about the topic we are teaching so we can be sure to handle them in the training.
2. **Check understanding:** *During training*, check understanding of the most critical concepts to make sure understanding is accurate.

Because everyone has different prior knowledge, we *expect* to find misconceptions and will need to take time to fix them. This is what instruction is all about. We will find out typical misconceptions by asking questions. If you are a subject-matter expert, ask yourself:
- What do people typically get wrong about this topic?
- What do people too often misunderstand about this topic?

If you are a subject-matter expert, *don't stop there.* You probably don't remember what it was like being new or newer to learning what you know. Ask people who are solid performers—and those who are newer to the work—what they misunderstood at first.

If you design instructional materials for others, ask these same questions of solid performers as well as people who are newer to the job. Don't ask a single subject-matter expert, as they often forget how to get from novice to expert. Thanks to Mirjam Neelen for reminding me about Guy Wallace's insights about not counting on a single subject-matter expert (see: https://eppic.biz/2009/09/02/beware-the-sme-interviewobservation-love-your-sme-but-dont-trust-them-1-on-1/).

We discuss instructional tactics for finding and fixing misconceptions in Tactic 24.

Tactic 6: Find Out What Gets in the Way

The last two tactics in this chapter help you find out things that can get in the way of successful learning and application. Think of it this way. You want to buy shades for your house. You pick out your favorite fabrics and the sales rep measures your windows and orders the shades. They come back in four weeks to install your blinds and they look great and fit perfectly.

Everything is perfect, right? Not so fast.

When you get up the next morning and go into your kitchen to make coffee, you see your nosy neighbor watching you through your too-sheer shades. Why didn't the salesperson recommend a less-sheer fabric? Or a light-blocking backing? On Saturday, when you want to sleep in, the light in your bedroom wakes you with the sun. Why hadn't the salesperson recommended fabrics that better block the morning sun? You had been happy but are now furious. The salesperson should have guided you better!

This example came to mind because I did work with a company that trains their salespeople to make sure their customers consider more than just aesthetics when selecting window coverings. Needs such as light, pets and children, and more influence the choice of the best window covering for a given window. It's the same thing with training. If other things derail the training, that's a terrible loss!

You might think it's not your problem to worry about things that can interfere with training outcomes. Here's why it is. Just like the woman who realized her shades didn't meet her needs, stakeholders will wonder why training outcomes are poor. They don't know what gets in the way. You must.

Work environment is the biggest issue

We must find out:
- Can/could people do this now?
- If not, why not?

In other words, we need to know: What does or will get in the way of doing this task? Table 4.4 shows work and individual factors that impact performance in the workplace.

Table 4.4 Factors that affect performance in the workplace (from Patti Shank's Performance Analysis course, Adapted from Carl Binder's [1998] Six Boxes™ model, *Performance Improvement*, 43[8].)

	Factors	Description
Work environment factors	1. Expectations and feedback	Clear standards of expected performance and feedback on performance
	2. Tools and resources	Access to tools and information needed to perform
	3. Consequences and incentives	Monetary and nonmonetary consequences and incentives, intended or not, that encourage people to perform in one manner over another.
	4. Process and work environment	Process factors including obstacles and barriers. Setting and ergonomic factors.
Individual factors	5. Skills	Skills an individual can use toward needed outcomes.
	6. Traits	Personal and professional characteristics.
	7. Motivation	Commitment and value toward performing.
	8. Life	Conditions that affect work, such as finances, relationships, and living conditions.

Research shows that work environment factors are the most common factors that get in the way of doing most work tasks. It is oh-so-common to have tools that are inadequate, tools and processes that require tedious workarounds, incentives to do the *wrong* thing (such as slacking off so you aren't given more work), and processes that are convoluted because of power struggles and lack of accountability. I'm betting you can think of more than one of these situations.

Training solves only one of these performance issues—and that's #5: Skills. We train because people do not know how to do a task. If we teach them to do the task but the tools don't let them do it, training doesn't help much. If we train them how to do the task but the process for doing it is ridiculous or someone won't let it happen—or the tools make it a nightmare—it won't happen.

But how do we find out?

Let's say XYZ Safety Training staff travels to several construction job sites and notices more than a few workers standing on the top steps of their stepladders while working. (Remember? No standing at or near the very top of the ladder.) They see a few people working on extension ladders working more safely.

A safety trainer asks the foreman in each location why people are working at the top of their stepladders. They hear a variation on the same answer: They don't know and they don't tell people how to work. The trainer asks workers the same question and finds out there are relatively few extension ladders. Workers use what they have available to use. This is a #2 factor and perhaps a #4 factor from Table 4.4.

The way to find out what gets in the way is to watch and ask. In this case, ladder training is potentially lifesaving, but there are issues that must be addressed (availability of tools and perhaps safety coaching issues with foreman).

And there's another issue. If everyone knows they need a longer ladder to be safe—but can't use a longer ladder because they are unavailable—it may be more of a tools issue and less of a skills issue. (We should do a performance analysis, but that's another book.) I am making a complex situation simpler to help you learn.

Watch. Ask. Fix problems *and* build skills.

Tactic 7: Assess Support for Skills

Research by Eduardo Salas—Professor of Psychology at University of Central Florida—and fellow authors used meta-analyses (statistical methods for contrasting and combining results from multiple research studies) to determine how to design, deliver, and implement training as effectively as possible. Their research, *The Science of Training and Development in Organizations: What Matters in Practice*, is a gem of highly applicable and not-hard-to-decipher information about how we can improve outcomes from training.

One of the most important factors affecting training outcomes is the post-training environment.

- Does the supervisor support the trained skills?
- Does the work environment allow people to use trained skills?
- Are there things that get in the way of using trained skills? (This and the item before map with factors 1-4 in Table 4.4.)

As discussed in the other tactics in this chapter, we need to watch, listen, and ask questions. There's a good chance that, if you have done Tactics 1-6, you already know the answer to the three questions listed above. If the answers are no, work needs to be done to support the training. It's possible that training isn't needed or needs to be delayed or abandoned.

Support adds influence and capability. It's needed for success.

Try It

We have reached the end of the tactics for **Strategy 1: Understand the Job Context.** Select instruction you want—or someone has asked you—to build. Then use the tactics in this chapter (recapped below) to analyze the job context for this training.

Tactic 1	**Connect Learning Objectives to Job Tasks** Write learning objectives that reflect what people should DO (current or upcoming job tasks), not topics.
Tactic 2	**Analyze Conditions Under Which People Perform the Tasks** Understand the conditions under which the tasks are performed. Conditions help us understand what people do and how they do it.
Tactic 3	**Evaluate What Must Be Remembered and What Can Be Looked Up** Find out what people need to commit to memory and what they can look up. Where on the remembering continuum is this information?
Tactic 4	**Analyze Social Processes** What are the social learning and social processes needed for optimal work outcomes? Clarify the social processes and skills that make desired outcomes more likely. What processes and skills must be trained?
Tactic 5	**Find the Typical Misconceptions** How may prior knowledge affect how people view what they are learning? What are typical misconceptions people have about what they are learning?
Tactic 6	**Find Out What Gets in the Way** Find out how work environment and individual performance factors affect trained skills. What can we do to fix these issues so good training outcomes are possible?
Tactic 7	**Assess Support for Skills** Find out if there is adequate support for trained skills on the job. If not, find out how to increase support; otherwise, training should be delayed or abandoned.

Consider doing this exercise with a group of people so you can discuss the following with others:
- What was helpful, less helpful?
- What did you learn?
- Which parts of this exercise will you continue to use in the future?

CHAPTER 5

Strategy 2: Practice for Self-direction

Most people realize that getting a college degree or other credential *does not* give them all the skills they will ever need for a career. All manner of work—from accounting to fixing cars to medicine, veterinary, small business, and home electrical and plumbing—continually evolves. Technological and other changes are moving at a pace much faster than at any time in history. Self-direction, defined as the ability to identify your own learning needs, set learning goals, plan and implement learning, and evaluate outcomes, is more important than ever.

Research finds that we typically must learn to be self-directed. Schooling and higher education are mostly about learning what we are told to learn in the way we are told to learn it—but, on the job, especially when job skills are a moving target, being self-directed is at a premium.

The academic world calls identifying your learning needs and managing the process of learning to meet these needs "self-regulated learning." Traci Sitzmann, Assistant Professor of Management at the University of Colorado, did meta-analysis of self-regulated learning in training that helps us understand how it works in the workplace. The first component is that *goals* are the main trigger for self-direction. And, like working memory, our time, attention, and energy are limited resources. We must, therefore, manage our time, attention, and energy resources because—if we push too hard—we have less, not more.

Self-direction is most critical when people are learning on their own—and learning on one's own is the key part of learning inside organizations. Even when people learn in training, they must apply and extend their learning in the workplace. Formal workplace learning is a small part of how people stay knowledgeable and skilled. There are larger roles for learning practitioners and anyone who develops adult learning programs—including helping adults maintain self-direction and find and use valuable resources.

In this chapter, I'm going to discuss two specific tactics we can use to help people be more self-directed learners (Figure 5.1).

Figure 5.1 Tactics that help people become more self-directed learners

Tactic 8: Work Toward Specific, Difficult, and Attainable Goals
Tactic 9: Use Self-directed Learning Strategies

Tactic 8: Work Toward Specific, Difficult, and Attainable Goals

I stated earlier that a critical factor affecting learning self-direction is having specific goals. Edwin Locke, an American psychologist, who was a professor at the University of Maryland, pioneered research in work motivation and goal-setting for more than three decades. His long-term work on goal setting and its impact on work performance is widely used in industrial and organizational psychology and is heavily cited in his field.

Over three-plus decades of joint research, Edwin Locke and co-researcher Gary Latham of the University of Toronto found that the most difficult goals produced the highest levels of performance—as long as the goals were reachable. According to Locke and Latham, goals affect performance through four mechanisms, shown in Table 5.1.

Table 5.1 Four mechanisms by which goals increase action (adapted)

Mechanism	Description
Direction	Goals direct attention and effort toward activities that promote goals and away from activities that prevent goal achievement.
Effort	Bigger goals lead to more effort than smaller goals.
Persistence	Harder goals commonly lead to a *prolonged* effort.
Eagerness to continue	Knowledge and skill improvements lead to improved commitment.

Locke and Latham's research shows that some factors tend to increase or decrease attainment of goals, as shown in Table 5.2.

Table 5.2 Moderators that increase and decrease goal attainment

Increase goal attainment	Decrease goal attainment
Specific and difficult goals	Nonspecific goals or telling people to "do their best"
Assigned goals, with rationale	
Training and support to make goal attainment possible	Assigned goals, without rationale
	Arbitrary goals without training or support
Learning goals	
Feedback on errors	Performance goals

Specific goals offer people clear reference points. Without clear reference points, people do not know if they have reached the goal or how well they are doing. In much of the feedback research I read to write this book, researchers discussed letting people know frequently how they are doing toward meeting goals.

Research found that people could commit to assigned team and organizational goals if helped to understand the need. Assigned goals where people didn't understand the need led to lower performance. Participation in making goals wasn't as important as understanding the need. Learning goals, where people have goals to learn rather than strict performance goals, were more successful. Researchers speculated that strict performance goals while learning led to anxiety, which typically lowers performance rather than enhances it.

Figure 5.2 shows an example of the first slide in an introductory story in a digital safety course.

Figure 5.2 Introductory course story

The specific goal in this course includes learning and performing four technical tasks to better protect oneself from online identity theft and then doing these tasks on a schedule. The course supplies the training and support (reminders) to make attainment of the goal possible as well as feedback on reaching the course goals.

Tactic 9: Use Self-directed Learning Strategies

Research shows that certain strategies can help people become more self-directed learners because they add awareness of and control of how they learn. Figure 5.3 shows three self-direction steps we can use to build self-direction into learning.

Figure 5.3 Three self-direction steps: Plan, Monitor, Evaluate

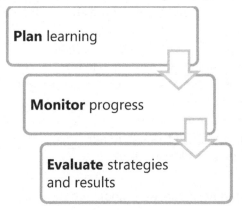

Using this three-step model will help you achieve better learning outcomes in any setting.

Self-direction questions

One of the easiest strategies is adding self-direction questions to instruction. Table 5.3 shows each of the steps with corresponding questions (that we can integrate into instruction). The planning questions naturally occur toward the beginning of a course or program. The monitoring questions are a natural for the middle of the course or any time it makes sense to stop and see how things are going. And the evaluation questions are a natural toward the end.

You may remember that I added some of these questions to Chapter 1 of this book so you could analyze your specific learning needs while reading this book.

Table 5.3 Three self-direction steps and related questions

Plan learning	• What are your specific goals? • Why are these goals important? • What resources and tools will you need? • What help will you need? • How will you get enough practice? • How will you track progress?
Monitor progress	• What are you confused about? • What problems are you having? • What do you need to know more about? (How can you find out?) • Are you learning what you need to learn? • How are you applying what you learn?
Evaluate strategies and results	• What worked well for you? Less well? (What might work better?) • What are your next steps? • What do you need to keep going? • What feedback do you need?

As you read this book and have questions about what you are reading, I would urge you to make notes about questions you have, things that aren't clear to you, and issues you want to know more about. You can write them in the margins. Or use the blank pages I added at the end of the book.

Question: Are you urging people to take more responsibility for their own knowledge and skills? Is that intentional?

Answer: That's absolutely intentional. We want to learn how to become more self-directed and have better learning outcomes from their individual learning efforts. We have a responsibility to understand and plan instruction to fit their needs (Strategy 1). But it's impossible to fulfill every possible need. A good part of the work must occur outside the narrow confines of training.

Self-direction activities

We can build in activities so people and workgroups can plan, monitor, and evaluate how they self-direct their learning. Table 5.4 shows example activities for each stage.

Table 5.4 Three self-direction steps and individual and collaborative self-directed learning activities

	Individual	*Teams*
Plan learning	Create specific and meaningful goals Clarify the importance of meeting these goals Develop an individual learning plan to meet the goals Find resources and tools Decide how to track progress Find people who can help	Create participation process to support team processes Create specific and meaningful goals Align goals to team and organizational goals Clarify the importance of meeting these goals Develop a team learning plan to meet the goals Find resources and tools Decide how to track progress Figure out how team members can help each other
Monitor progress	Reflect on insights and application to work Track questions Track progress Analyze and solve problems Find other resources and tools Get help with time management	Reflect on insights and application to work Track questions Track progress Encourage exchange of ideas, insights, problems Analyze and solve problems Find other resources and tools Help each other with time management
Evaluate strategies and results	Analyze challenges Choose next steps Get feedback	Analyze challenges Choose next steps Offer team feedback

Question: Why would I add self-directed learning activities in a formal training session? Seems mixed up.

Answer: I can think of three primary reasons for adding self-directed learning activities to a formal training situation. (You may think of more.):

- There is always more to learn. Training is often limited (in content and duration), but life and work will supply many related reasons to learn.
- We should model how to keep learning and how to learn when formal training isn't available.
- The continual shifting of skills means this role (supporting self-directed learning) is becoming essential and we should embrace it.

Try It

We have reached the end of the tactics for **Strategy 2: Practice for Self-direction**. Select instruction you want—or someone has asked you—to build. Then use the tactics in this chapter (recapped below) to add practice elements that teach people to be more self-directed.

Tactic 8	**Work Toward Specific, Difficult, and Attainable Goals** Develop learning goals that • Are specific and difficult • Have a clear rationale • Are attainable with the provided training • Focus on learning • Offer feedback that helps people know how they are doing toward goals
Tactic 9	**Use Self-directed Learning Strategies** Use self-directed questions and individual or collaborative strategies to help people and teams plan, monitor, and evaluate their learning. Create learning paths instead of learning events by adding self-directed learning activities.

Consider doing this exercise with a group of people so you can discuss the following with others:
- What was helpful, less helpful?
- What did you learn?
- Which parts of this exercise will you continue to use in the future?

CHAPTER 6

Strategy 3: Practice for Transfer

One of the biggest challenges for adult learning is transferring what people learn during instruction to where it needs to be applied—typically on the job. Too many people who develop instruction assume that, if they teach it, it will transfer. But transfer from instruction to the workplace is difficult. It's important that we design specifically for transfer so it is more likely to occur.

Much of the research-oriented insight in this chapter comes from Rebecca Grossman's and Eduardo Salas's evidence-based guidance on training transfer. Rebecca Grossman is an Assistant Professor in Industrial/Organizational Psychology at Hofstra University.

The transfer research is not always easy to understand—and, like the feedback research, there are areas of disagreement. Grossman and Salas summed up some great insights in their work, and give advice adult learning practitioners will find easy to understand and follow. Figure 6.1 shows the tactics I'll be discussing in Strategy 3.

Figure 6.1 Tactics that help people practice for transfer

Tactic 10: Make Training Relevant
Tactic 11: Build Practice that Mirrors Work
Tactic 12: Show the Right *and* Wrong Ways
Tactic 13: Train How to Handle Errors
Tactic 14: Include Whole-skill Practice
Tactic 15: Help with Post-training Support

Tactic 10: Make Training Relevant

The issue of relevance appears repeatedly throughout this book because research says relevance is one of the most important issues for adult participants. We begin with Tactic 1: Connect Learning Objectives to Job Tasks, where we intentionally connect instruction to what people do on the job.

Research tells us it is easier for people to more actively engage when they see a specific and important purpose for the challenges of learning, practicing, using feedback to improve, and applying what they learn. Relevance creates the environment for transfer. This is because people must decide training is worthwhile and worth applying. Participants can relate to training on various levels:

- Personal
- Group
- Organizational

Personal

We can help people relate instructional objectives and content to their lives and work. There are various instructional activities that help people openly connect course content to their personal lives or work.

1. Ask questions about how training applies to them and their life or work
2. Ask people to discuss the real-life challenges and benefits of what they are learning
3. Ask what people already know about what we are discussing
4. Ask people to share personal stories relevant to the content
5. Tell a story and ask for insights about it

Figure 6.2 shows an activity from a virtual classroom session asking participants to add their own objectives for the course. Karen Hyder, a master virtual classroom coach and my co-facilitator on joint trainings, uses this virtual classroom technique and others shown in this chapter.

Figure 6.2 Activity from a virtual classroom session, add personal objectives

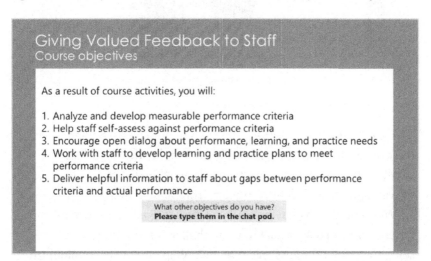

Figure 6.3 shows another slide from the virtual classroom session that helps participants relate to the content via a story. It's the beginning of a video that shows a typical, but unproductive feedback session between Carol, the supervisor, and Kenny, one of her staff members.

Figure 6.3 Activity from a virtual classroom session, add insights

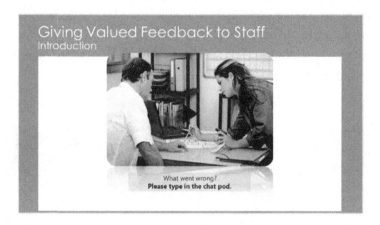

Figure 6.4 shows another approach to helping participants find their own relevance. Sometimes we downplay the negatives of a situation but, believe me, participants are thinking of the negatives—so we might as well deal with them front and center.

When discussing having staff self-assess against performance criteria, we can ask people to offer challenges and benefits of the self-assessment process. We may follow up with ways to minimize the challenges.

Figure 6.4 Activity from a virtual classroom session, add challenges and benefits

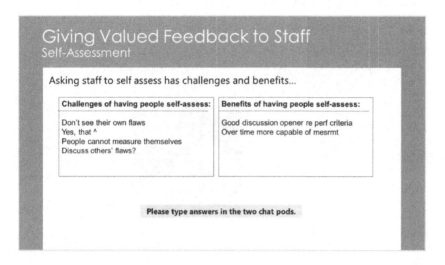

Group

We can use similar techniques to help people see the relevance for their work group, family, or other group—depending on the subject matter. For example, in training for home childcare providers, we analyzed what was most important to the providers, the children in their care, and the children's families. Using this knowledge shaped content and activities (practice) that were far more relevant to participant needs.

Organizational

For organizational relevance, we need to understand how the training fits into organizational needs. We can use questions, stories, and shared insights to discuss them so people understand how the training is relevant.

For example, Figure 6.5 shows two pages from a food safety course that tells the story of the three-month shut-down of Zina's restaurant after an outbreak of foodborne illness. The first page offers a video about the problem (how and why it happened) and its effect on the victims, the owner, and the staff. The second page asks participants to consider why this event occurred.

Figure 6.5 Online activity about experience with foodborne illness

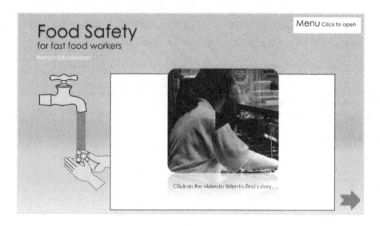

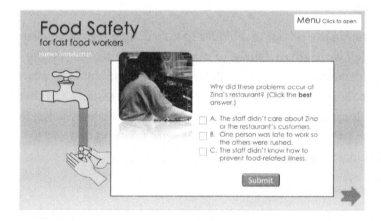

Tactic 11: Build Practice that Mirrors Work

Grossman and Salas discuss a recurring theme in research about how realistic environments improve transfer from instruction to work. Practice should have the same **environmental cues, consequences, variability, and social interactions** as work. Let's consider each of these factors and how they can improve transfer.

Environmental cues

Research shows that environmental cues can help training transfer from instruction to work because, when people are at work, those same cues remind them to do what they learned in training. For example, training for safety in the warehouse means paying attention to the work going on around you, to signs, and to noises. Figure 6.6 shows an environmental cue that tells workers that forklifts could be nearby and they have the right-of-way.

Figure 6.6 One environmental cue that forklifts may be working in the area

Research shows that using the same safety cues in training as in the workplace prompts use of safety skills in the workplace. Remember, we do not want to bombard anyone's perception or overload their thinking—especially while they are learning. So we should select environmental cues most important to training results.

For safety training, as an example, environmental cues are likely to be different in different environments. On a construction site, certain noises or lack of noises tell others there is a problem. In a bank, the lack of noise or presence of alarms indicate danger.

Question: To make training feel like work, should we assume training scenarios should always look exactly like the real work situation?

Answer: This is an important (but difficult-to-answer) question—and the answer has to do with *fidelity*. So, rather than give you a simple answer, I'm going to go into a bit of detail. Because it really is an important issue. Especially since I repeatedly discuss making training like work so it is more relevant, memorable (easy to remember), and transferable.

Fidelity

Fidelity (as I am using the term) means the extent to which training matches critical elements of the job environment. The research I used here discussed training simulations and training games—but this information applies to training environments in general, too. I describe the critical elements, or types of fidelity, in Table 6.1.

Table 6.1 Elements or types of training fidelity

Elements	Description
Physical	How much training looks, sounds, and feels like the job
Functional	How much training acts like the job (generally used for how things work, such as tools and systems)
Cognitive	How much training requires people to think like they will think on the job
Psychological	How much training induces similar emotional responses as on the job, such as time pressure, stress, or conflict
Physiological	How much training induces similar physical responses as the job, such as pain

One obvious question: Which types of fidelity are beneficial? And are any types detrimental? Research shows that fidelity can be beneficial for transfer, but fidelity can also be overwhelming and make it harder to learn—especially when the type and amount of fidelity are not valuable. This should not surprise us: We know we can feel overloaded by too much content.

Researchers explain that we must prioritize fidelity based on required training outcomes. Take these training objectives for a module on putting out small office fires.

1. Decide if the fire is small enough to put out using a fire extinguisher.
2. If the fire is small enough, get the fire extinguisher quickly and put it out.
3. If the fire is larger or is spreading, get everyone out of the building and call the fire department.

Which type(s) of fidelity is/are most critical to the learning objectives above? Please write down your answers before continuing. The answer is on the next page, but you will learn more by thinking through this issue than by jumping right to the answer!

> Patti's answer:
>
> **The types of fidelity I think are *most* important are** cognitive and psychological fidelity. Physical fidelity may be important if people do not know where the fire extinguishers are or how to use them. Cognitive fidelity is critical because the main problem is deciding if the fire is small enough to put out. Psychological fidelity is also important because of time pressure. Fires can go from small to large quickly.
>
> **How does this match with your thoughts? Did you have different assumptions that led to different answers?**

Because the right kinds of fidelity aid transfer—but too much can be overwhelming—we should analyze the types of fidelity most needed for a given training situation. In most soft skills training situations, for instance, the desired training outcomes are primarily cognitive. We want people to figure out the right thing(s) to do. As a result, physical fidelity isn't needed; but, if there is time pressure or there are certain kinds of stress, we should add those types of fidelity in with variability of practice, which I discuss later in this Tactic.

Consequences

In Chapter 3, we discussed the differences between intrinsic (internal) and extrinsic (external) feedback. The consequences of actions are intrinsic feedback and they can be very powerful and memorable.

If possible, allow people to realize the actual results of their work. Rather than saying what is wrong and why, it helps people if they learn to interpret consequences. When the copier jams, we get an error message. Can we interpret it and fix the jam? When we ask someone for help and they turn us down, can we interpret their signals? Being able to interpret less-than-obvious messages is an important work skill.

In Tactic 5, we analyze typical misconceptions so we can then use them in practice scenarios. We saw an example of using real mistakes in Zina's restaurant closing video. In a buzzed drinking scenario in Figure 6.7, we see the use of a misconception that it's legal to drive after drinking if under the legal blood alcohol level.

Figure 6.7 Two screens from a buzzed driving scenario

The next scene shows a consequence of the *wrong* choice (intrinsic feedback).

Both scenes in Figure 6.7 add physical fidelity but they aren't really needed. Cognitive fidelity (thought process) and psychological fidelity (emotions and stressors) are the main issues. Because the pictures are static and dark, they don't add much distraction. But we might want to test them against a text-only scenario to see which works better.

One of the great things about knowing what science tells us works is that we can spend our time and effort on the things that make the most difference.

Question: If we need to make training like work, why not simply train at work?

Answer: A great deal of informal and formal training happens at work because all the things needed to practice are there: tools, people, and work tasks. But, sometimes, we must train people offline because the work is either too complex or the work has legal, regulatory, or danger considerations. For example, we aren't going to teach people what to do about safe driving when drunk. They need to know before.

Variability

Research by Salas and others tells us we need to help people practice under the range of conditions they will face on the job. Too much training uses one or two practice situations only. We train to improve confidence and skill. This means people need to practice in the likely range of typical situations until proficient in those situations. If there are less-likely situations where people must be proficient, these must be practiced and skills must be maintained. I discuss the issue of skill maintenance in Tactic 20.

Tactic 2 asks us to analyze the conditions under which people use the skills on the job. For a course in giving performance feedback, for example, we might find there are typical unhelpful reactions and it is hard to deal with them. Common unhelpful reactions may include anxiety, anger, defensiveness, and not listening to the feedback.

PRACTICE AND FEEDBACK FOR DEEPER LEARNING • 95

Knowing these conditions helps us build realistic scenarios (Figure 6.8) that participants can use to gain confidence and skill in the variability of responses.

Figure 6.8 Numerous scenarios to mirror realistic conditions

Question: The training I am building has a lot of potential variability—especially with diverse types of customers and unique needs. I was going to concentrate on the most common customer type and most common need. But I'm thinking this may short-change staff skills. How do I improve their skills and transfer without making the training too long?

Answer: See if you can organize skill needs by customer type or customer needs. Then you can build different versions for staff who need different versions. You can likely reuse much of the content.

Social interactions

Realistic practice should include social interactions that affect the outcomes of work. In training practice, we too often train people like they do everything alone and are the only ones affecting their work tasks.

We should also embed realistic social interactions, such as getting sign-offs, asking questions, getting advice and help, and needed discussions.

The training shown in Figure 6.8 involves obvious social interactions. But many tasks involve less-obvious social interactions we might forget to include in training—but that affect task outcomes. Table 6.2 shows social interactions in the right column that affect the outcomes of the tasks or decisions shown in the left column.

Table 6.2 Social interactions for various tasks or decisions

Task or decision	Applicable social interactions
Picking the right ladder for the job	Asking a co-worker to borrow his or her equipment
Changing passwords	Asking IT for help
Driving "buzzed"	Getting the keys from your friend
Driving "buzzed"	Interacting with law enforcement

We can choose to say, "Ask a co-worker if you can borrow his or her equipment," or say, "Ask IT for help if you cannot do this yourself." "Take the keys from your friend." But the outcome depends on *how well* the social interaction occurs. For example, in Figure 6.9, we use a scenario to practice HOW to ask a co-worker to borrow his or her ladder.

PRACTICE AND FEEDBACK FOR DEEPER LEARNING • 97

Figure 6.9 Social interaction scenario

Figure 6.10 shows another way of handling the social interactions of a specific task—people asking for their own or a family member's medical records. The video explains to this audience (medical receptionists) the rules about requests for medical records. The FAQs dig a bit deeper into some of the most frequently asked questions about these rules.

Figure 6.10 Social interaction issues embedded in video, FAQs, and exercises

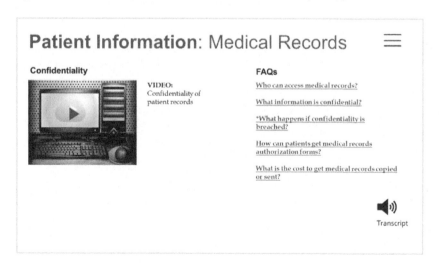

Resource

One of the ways to add fidelity to training is through scenarios. Cathy Moore has a scenario design course that I highly recommend. You can learn more about it at cathy-moore.com.

Tactic 12: Show the Right *and* Wrong Ways

Training commonly shows the right way to perform or behave. For example, Figure 6.11 shows a screen that describes and shows the right way to explain how to access a patient's medical records— including telling patients or family members what they should do.

Figure 6.11 The right way to explain accessing medical records

Behavior modeling is a highly-regarded and well-researched strategy for behavior-based training interventions. That's why so many use this kind of training for customer service, supervisory, communication, and related skills. Behavior-modeling training has four steps. The video in Figure 6.11 models the first two steps of this process.

1. Describe the behavior
2. Model the behavior
3. Practice the behavior
4. Supply feedback

An often-cited 2005 meta-analysis of the effects of behavior-modeling training found that training transfer was greatest when participants see not just the positive model but *both* positive and negative models. The training was updated (Figure 6.12) to include and analyze a positive model and a negative model.

Figure 6.12 Correct and incorrect way to explain accessing medical records

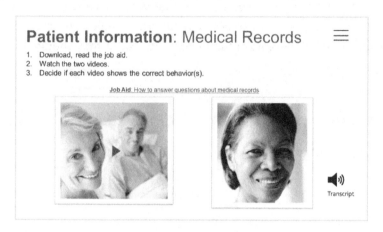

To make sure participants understand the right way to perform the skills, Figure 6.13 shows three practice cases. Each case asks how well the process was explained and what, if anything, was left out. The three cases also include variability: your child's records, your own records, and another medical provider's records.

Figure 6.13 Practice activity

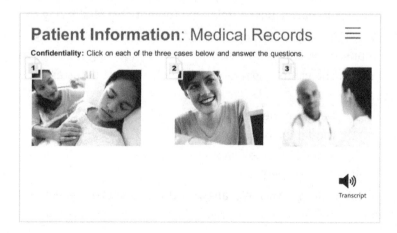

Tactic 13: Train How to Handle Errors

Mirroring realistic work environments helps with transfer and errors are part of work. Therefore, it improves transfer when we train people how to handle errors. Error handling training may include
- Common errors
- Serious errors
- Diagnosing errors
- How to handle errors

Figure 6.14 shows an activity that helps people analyze common error messages when filing travel expenses.

Figure 6.14 Error handling activity

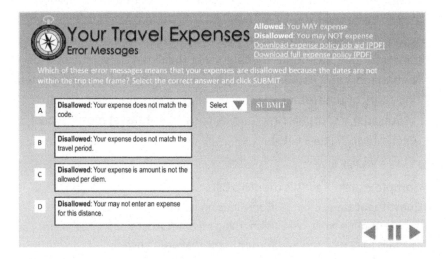

Error training helps people understand errors, helps them prepare for errors, and often improves the perceived relevance of training.

Tactic 14: Use Whole-skill Practice

Many times, when training complex skills, we break it up into its constituent parts to make it simpler to teach, learn, and practice. Earlier instructional design models often advocated for this approach to avoid cognitive overload from tasks that were too complex. But they eventually combined individual tasks so people had the opportunity to practice the whole task.

Increasingly—as complex skills are not simply the sum of their parts—research evidence has shown the importance of how knowledge and skills are organized and integrated. Recent models focus on whole-task approaches that embed the organization and integration of constituent skills. Research shows that these models lead to better transfer from training to the workplace. The research in this area comes primarily from Jeroen J. G. Van Merriënboer (Professor of Educational Technology at the Open University of the Netherlands) and Paul Kirschner (Professor of Psychology at the Open University of the Netherlands).

Consider a complex task (and its constituent tasks) most do on a regular basis (Figure 6.15).

Figure 6.15 Pay bills

Complex task: Pay this month's bills

Constituent tasks	Coordination issues
1. Determine what bills to pay	Is anything missing? Are there any bills I am forgetting or that aren't here?
2. Verify due dates	Will I get more money during the month that will allow me to pay more on bills due later?
3. Crunch the numbers and decide amounts	Can I pay these off? What amounts can I pay?

Figure 6.15 shows just a few of the coordination issues in the right column. Paying bills might have three constituent tasks, but those tasks require close organization and coordination among them. Each

task impacts the others and requires coordination. For example, if I don't see one of the bills, I might think I have more money and pay off another bill. Then, if I find the first bill, I might not have enough money to pay it—causing additional problems. In complex tasks, there are typically many organizational and coordination issues. When we teach the skills separately, these may not be obvious.

People best transfer to the job what they learn from training when we train using whole-skill practice—not by breaking practice into constituent parts and only practicing the parts. The coordination and integration of the parts is a crucial element and, too often, we act like it isn't part of the process. But it is a critical part of the process and of success.

Make complex tasks easier to learn

One of the best ways to give people whole-task practice that is not overwhelming is to have people practice *simpler versions* of the whole task and work toward more complex versions of the whole task over time. Figure 6.16 shows two examples of practicing simpler versions of whole tasks and progressing to more complex versions of the whole tasks.

Figure 6.16 Complex tasks, simpler to more complex

Whole Task:	Track your family spending in Microsoft® Excel®	Decorate with mosaics
simpler	• Track coffee purchases	• Build a mosaic trivet
↕	• Track clothing spending by person over three months	• Build a mosaic platter
more complex	• Track family spending by family member and category over calendar year	• Build a mosaic table top

The simpler whole tasks in Figure 6.16 use the same knowledge base as the more complex whole tasks. While participants are learning constituent skills (Excel budgets: worksheets, formulas, AutoSum, column width, and so forth), they are learning them in context and seeing how the constituent tasks affect each other and work together.

You may also add constituent tasks over time. This is another way to hold complexity down while still allowing people to work with whole, real tasks that keep the coordination and integration elements. For instance, as people become used to basic Excel tasks, we might add formatting and layout tasks.

Start with more support

Another research finding about helping complex skills transfer from training to the workplace is that it is helpful to offer more support to start and then reduce support as people can perform on their own. Here are some types of support we can provide to help people as they are starting to learn:

- Starting sets and templates
- Task demonstrations
- Models and diagrams
- Examples of the task performed under variable conditions
- Job aids

For the Excel budget task, as an example, we might develop software demonstrations showing how to perform the first task. We might offer job aids for common tasks (worksheets, common formulas, formatting, and so on).

When to use part practice

There are some instances where we will use part practice. This normally in the following situation:
- The task is very complex (has many, many steps)
- The steps must be done correctly
- The people are new to the task (there is a high likelihood of being overwhelmed)

In these cases, we use part practice (practicing the constituent parts of the whole skill individually) to make sure people can do the individual parts without error and then move on to other parts. We typically make sure people can do all the parts and offer support tools (videos, job aids, guides, and so forth).

An example of a situation where part practice might logically be used is teaching patients to give themselves insulin using a syringe (Table 6.3). It has many task groups—and the subtasks have many parts. Each part of each task group is very important. The task groups may be taught separately and then brought together to lower cognitive load.

Table 6.3 Complex task groups within a complex task

Task group	Subtasks
1. Gather supplies	a. Wash your hands b. Get the correct insulin bottle, correct syringe, and alcohol swab
2. Get the correct dosage of insulin ready to inject	a. Make sure you have the correct insulin and syringe b. Determine how many IUs of insulin to inject c. Wipe the top of the insulin bottle with the alcohol swab d. Roll the insulin bottle, if needed e. Get the proper syringe ready f. Pull the plunger of the syringe down to the correct dosage units g. Push the needle of the syringe into the insulin bottle

		h.	Push the plunger of the syringe down
		i.	Pull the plunger of the syringe back to the correct dosage units
		j.	Remove air bubbles
		k.	Check to see if the dosage is correct
3.	Prepare to inject the insulin	a.	Pinch up injection site using the correct technique
		b.	Wipe with alcohol swab
		c.	Push needle into skin
		d.	Push syringe plunger in
		e.	Pull syringe plunger out
		f.	Remove syringe
4.	Dispose of needle properly	a.	Clip off the needle
		b.	Place needle in a sharps container
5.	Store supplies		Place supplies back in storage

NOTE: *This example illustrates a complex skill with multiple substeps only. I am not a healthcare provider and the list may not be complete or accurate.*

Tactic 15: Help with Post-training Support

The research of Salas and others shows that others' support for trained skills on the job heavily influences whether trained skills transfer to the job. When people get back to the job and supervisors or peers say something akin to, "That's not how we do it here"—or they do things differently from how skills were trained—people will likely *not* apply to the job what they learned in training. If anything, quite the opposite.

We *need* supervisors and peers to support trained skills on the job. Research says support for trained skills includes
- Short- and long-term skill goals
- Debriefing trained skills
- The chance to practice trained skills
- Observing others using trained skills

What is our role, as developers of instruction, in making this support happen? Supervisors and others have many other tasks to do and supporting training is often not on their minds—even if we would like it to be. But we can help them support training by making it easier. One of the most productive ways to help supervisors and team leads support training is to build and offer appropriate post-training support items. And because these people aren't used to using them, we may need to market them and possibly find some internal champions for using them in their departments.

Figure 6.17 shows an example of post-training debrief questions developed for after an online privacy course.

Figure 6.17 Example debrief questions

> **Online Privacy** Debrief Questions
>
> 1. Is there anything *you* will do differently to keep your personal information safe?
> 2. Is there anything you think *we* should do differently to keep staff personal information safe?
> 3. Are there tasks you need to practice from the course? When will you be able to practice?
> 4. Do you need any additional help?

Figure 6.18 shows an example of a checklist developed for and with department supervisors to match job tasks and then support job tasks after training. Supervisors can use the checklist to make sure inexperienced staff have adequate practice with clusters of specific selling skills after training. After training on the skills their salespeople were learning, they understood that sales skills took a great deal of practice—and that training was only the start of building these skills.

Figure 6.18 Example task checklist

Selling Tasks Checklist

1

Completed	Tasks
	Ask questions to uncover needs
	Ask price sensitivity questions
	Show applicable items and present features and benefits for selected purpose
	Ask for input on items

2

Completed	Skill
	Ask questions to uncover wants and wishes
	Add items beyond customer's stated price range
	Compare benefits of lower- and higher-priced items
	Ask for questions

3

Completed	Skill
	Explain process for custom orders
	Give two possible delivery dates
	Set-up measure

In Tactic 7: Assess Support for Skills, we assessed if the skills we want to teach are supported on the job. If they aren't supported, we have a problem that needs fixing *before* anyone should consider developing and implementing training. Perhaps current tools don't support trained skills—or the workarounds are far too burdensome. We may be able to help with the problematic situation or it may be above our pay grade. Regardless, it's a red flag.

There are also situations where supervisors are busy and don't know how to support it. This is where we can use our knowledge to offer tools to make supporting these skills easier.

Try It

We have reached the end of the tactics for Strategy 3: Practice for Transfer. Select instruction you want—or someone has asked you—to build. Then use the tactics in this chapter (recapped below) to add practice elements that improve transfer.

Tactic 10	**Make Training Relevant** Make sure to know and embed the specific and important purposes for the challenges of learning, practicing, using to feedback to improve, and applying what people learn during training. Relevance = engagement.
Tactic 11	**Build Practice that Mirrors Work** Use environmental cues, fidelity, consequences, variability, and social interactions to make training like work in the ways that count the most. However, to not overwhelm people, analyze which ways are most critical.
Tactic 12	**Show the Right *and* Wrong Ways** Error training helps people understand errors, prepare for errors, and often improves the perceived relevance of training.
Tactic 13	**Train How to Handle Errors** Training in error handling has been shown to improve transfer
Tactic 14	**Use Whole-skill Practice** When teaching complex skills, start with simpler whole-skill practice, and move towards more complex whole skill practice. Training skills as constituent skills leaves out the coordination and integration tasks necessary to performing complex skills.
Tactic 15	**Help with Post-training Support** Help supervisors and team leaders support trained skills by building post-training support items useful to support the training objectives long term.

CHAPTER 7

Strategy 4: Practice for Remembering

In Strategy 3, I discussed one of the harder learning challenges: building practice that helps people transfer what they learn in instruction to where it needs to be applied—in the workplace (or elsewhere in the real world). Another large challenge for learning is practice so they can remember important knowledge and skills from instruction. Too many people who build instruction assume people will remember. But forgetting is common and remembering is more likely if we design for it.

In Tactic 3, I discussed the need to evaluate what must be remembered and what can be looked up. In this chapter, I'll discuss designing instruction that helps people remember what must be remembered. I'll also discuss what we can do to help people keep remembering. Figure 7.1 shows the tactics for Strategy 4.

Figure 7.1 Tactics that help people practice for the remembering they need to do on the job

Tactic 16: Use Real Context(s)
Tactic 17: Use Self-explanations
Tactic 18: Space Learning and Remembering
Tactic 19: Support Memory with Memory Aids
Tactic 20: Support Essential Skill Upkeep

Question: Wait—we need to support remembering after instruction?

Answer: Without regular use, memory and skill decay (fade). And decay makes it harder to recall and use what you know. So we will also want to help people maintain knowledge and skills—especially critical ones.

Tactic 16: Use Real Context(s)

Research shows that memory is context sensitive. What this means is we remember context along with memory. This is one of the reasons it's easy to remember where you were or how you felt when you hear a song from your past—and one of the reasons why making sure we embed the context during instruction can make it easier for us to transfer trained skills to the workplace.

When I was young and training to be a bank teller, the trainers trained all job skills in the context of the job. For example, we completed deposit and withdrawal transactions exactly as we would do it on the job, including what to say to the customer. We used the same tools we would use on the job so, when we began to use them, they would be familiar and remind us of what we had learned in training.

To make it easier for learning to transfer to the job context—and to remember what we learn—it's critical that we use real job contexts during instruction. Simply, when people are trained in their new knowledge and skills using job context, they remember and use them better than they do without context.

Consider an example from banking and retail that we see regularly: Counting change back on a purchase with cash. Cash registers often tell workers how much change to give the customer, so many no longer know how to count change back. But, since digital tools are subject to problems and electricity failures, this is a basic skill most people who deal with money and customers should know. Figure 7.2 shows the process.

Figure 7.2 Process for counting change back from a cash purchase

Counting Change Back to a Customer

Example: Customer's purchase comes to $12.82 and she gives you a $20 bill

What to do	**Count aloud into customer's hand or onto the counter**
1. First, count coins *up* to the nearest dollar ($13): three pennies (= $12.85), one nickel (= $12.90), and one dime (= $13.00).	"That's $12.85, $12.90, $13.00."
2. Next, count dollar bills *up* to the dollar amount the customer gave you: two one-dollar bills (= $15.00), and one five-dollar bill (= $20.00).	"That's $15.00 and five makes $20.00."

How might we train this skill to new retail clerks? Stop for a moment and think about the tactics we've discussed so far as well as this tactic. What would help people learn this skill deeply? Please write down your answers before continuing. The answer is on the next page, but you will learn more by thinking through this issue than jumping right to the answer!

> Patti's answer:
>
> Here are some ways I would make this practice activity relevant and transferable. I would analyze the situations in which change is given to customers so that I could design practice that is most like the real situations. Then I would design practice using a variety of realistic situations, working from simple to complex situations (such as giving change back from a dollar to giving change back from $50). I would design practice for both the social aspects and making errors. I would build post-training support materials for supervisors to make sure training skills are supported on the job.
>
> Was your answer similar? If not, what assumptions did you have that might have been different from Patti's?

Training or teaching in context (how knowledge is applied) improves encoding in long-term memory and retrieval when needed from long-term memory. When memory is encoded with context, it is easier to remember.

Because falls from ladders on construction sites can have devastating results—including permanent disability and loss of life—the training session added final on-the-job safety sessions where instructors (construction safety experts) go to the job sites and create some hazardous situations and ask participants to work together to make them safe.

By working with construction foremen to understand potential worksite ladder safety hazards—and building in the variety of potentially unsafe situations crew members deal with—people use the real context, including the social context of needing to share equipment and ask for help.

A real context helps technical training sessions, too. Figure 7.3 shows a screen from an online privacy course. Participants have alternatives for setting up a password and getting authentication codes (process to verify user identity) in the pages prior to the page shown. This page uses the password and code to move to the next page. The point is that the training doesn't just show and tell authentication—people perform the steps.

Figure 7.3 Practice page from data safety course

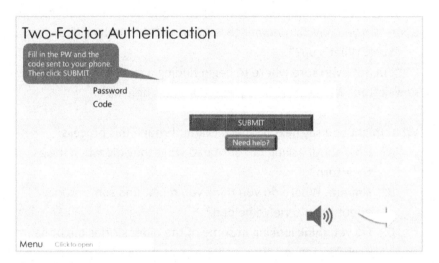

One of the challenges people commonly bring up when I discuss making training relevant and real is the difficulty of recreating real practice situations in an online environment.

There are two separate issues here. One of the issues is whether we must have all practice in online courses occur online. The other issue is whether all the online practice must be high fidelity.

Practice in the real job context does not have to take place online—even in online courses. We can have online courses that have offline practice elements. For example, if participants are learning how to coach a staff member, they can practice those discussions with their own staff. When Gene asks if you can help him think through how to find more donors, you can begin to practice on the job by saying, "Gene, walk me through the ideas you've had."

While we can build realistic scenarios for practice, typically the most important factor when it comes to fidelity (realism), is psychological or cognitive fidelity—not physical fidelity. I discussed fidelity in Tactic 11. You can build a coaching scenario that includes the psychological and cognitive fidelity but not the physical fidelity. It might start like Figure 7.4.

Figure 7.4 Text-based scenario

You're working on a document when Maria pops her head in your door. "Do you have a moment to help me with something?" she asks.

"Sure. What's up?"

"I'm not even sure where to begin finding a story for the newsletter," Maria says. "I've never done this before."

What might you say next to coach Maria through this process?
- A. How about asking Jan or Marco what they did when it was their turn?
- B. Hmmm. Where do you think you might find some stories about people we've helped?
- C. Do you think looking at some of the older stories might be useful?
- D. Let's brainstorm. You go first.

Figure 7.5 shows an example of using offline practice in an online course. The course developers understand the need for practice, giving feedback, and dealing with a variety of people and reactions. The course also includes scenarios, but it was difficult to build in enough variation. Using practice partners allowed them to add more variation.

Figure 7.5 Offline practice example

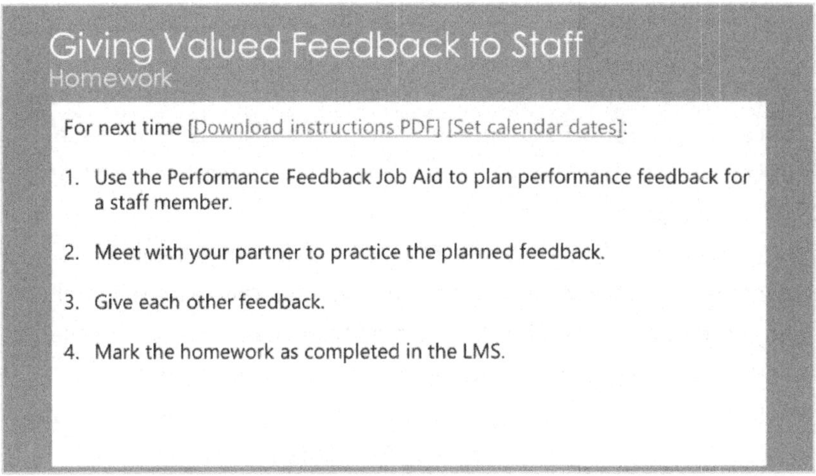

> **Giving Valued Feedback to Staff**
> Homework
>
> For next time [Download instructions PDF] [Set calendar dates]:
>
> 1. Use the Performance Feedback Job Aid to plan performance feedback for a staff member.
> 2. Meet with your partner to practice the planned feedback.
> 3. Give each other feedback.
> 4. Mark the homework as completed in the LMS.

Using real context(s) for application helps people remember and more easily apply what they are learning at work.

How can you add more real-world context to your upcoming projects?

Tactic 17: Use Self-explanations

In Chapter 2, where I explained the applicable science of learning concepts that apply to deeper learning, I asked you to write each concept in your own words. In learning sciences, we call this strategy "self-explanations."

Michelene Chi, Professor at the Institute for the Science of Teaching and Learning at Arizona State University—who researches and writes a great deal on the learning sciences—explains that self-explanations help us integrate new information with prior knowledge. When studying worked problems (problems where the process and answer are shown), self-explanations can help participants discover the best problem-solving methods.

A self-explanation, then, is an instructional strategy that asks participants to describe a concept or an issue and the meaning of the concept or issue in their own words. It helps them integrate what they are learning with what they already know, and make connections between what they are learning and what they know. In addition to using self-explanations to remember, they can be used in training to find out if there are problems with understanding or misconceptions.

A potential benefit of classroom or virtual classroom training over asynchronous (self-paced) training is having participants create content such as self-explanations. It is much more difficult to create answers, such as a self-explanation, than to pick the correct explanation from those shown on the screen.

Figure 7.6 shows ways to have people use self-explanations in a data safety course. As when writing good multiple-choice questions, the wrong answers must be plausible, not silly. In the bottom example of Figure 7.6, the incorrect answers (A and C) are plausible. A is a misconception of how two-step authentication works and C is a correct answer—but not for this question. Misconceptions and correct answers (but not for this question) make the best plausible incorrect answers.

Figure 7.6 Potential use of self-explanations in the data safety course

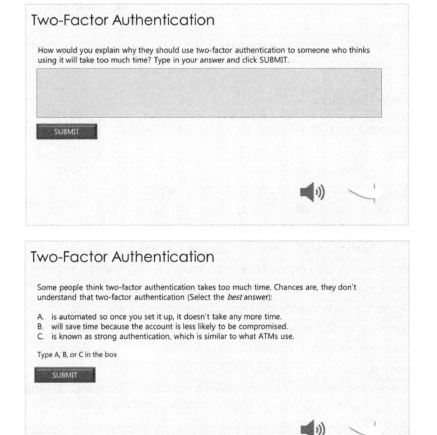

When people need to make their own sense, they often understand it better and remember it more.

How can you use self-explanations in your upcoming projects?

Tactic 18: Space Learning and Remembering

One of the top research results is spaced learning and spaced remembering (often called spaced repetition and spaced retrieval, respectively). I'll discuss what they are and how we might use them in training.

Spaced learning

Spaced learning refers to repeating (over time) the same learning presentation. The reason we should consider doing this is that research shows we more easily remember what we study when we study the same material several times for shorter periods of time (spaced learning) rather than studying the material one time for longer periods of time (massed learning).

Research generally finds that spaced learning is better for remembering than massed learning. Interestingly, massed learning produces better remembering than spaced learning right after presenting the content—and for a short time afterwards. So cramming works for answering questions on a test. But spaced learning is superior for remembering for the long run, and this is where it counts for remembering for use on the job.

Here's an obvious problem: Spaced learning takes more time than massed learning because breaking up content into several instructional and practice sessions takes more time or more sessions. Researchers explain how large an issue this may be for formal schooling but—since learning in organizations should ideally be fit around work—we can consider many ways to make this happen in training. I will shortly discuss just a few ways to make this happen; I imagine you can think of many more.

There are multiple reasons spacing learning over time works to resist forgetting of learned content. Here are a few reasons research describes:

- Increases mental effort, which improves remembering
- Facilitates better encoding in long-term memory
- Overcomes periods of inattentiveness during learning
- May offer varying coverage of the same topic, which gives our memory different "hooks" for remembering

Let's say we train a new group of customer service reps four times a year. And the training program is two months long. What do you think happens to what you trained in week two after you get to week four? [Cue *Jeopardy* music here.] That's right. They have forgotten much of what they learned earlier. This is true for anything we learn. People forget.

If we are going to train people to remember things they must remember (Tactic 2), we must have a plan in place to help them remember. Or help people put a plan into place to remember (Strategy 2). Forgetting essentially starts immediately if the knowledge is not used. Use it or lose it.

Table 7.1 shows an original training plan (left) and a possible spaced learning plan (right) to help people remember what they are learning.

Table 7.1 Initial and spaced learning training plans

Initial training plan	Spaced learning training plan
Week 1 Content	Week 1 Content
Week 2 Content	Week 2 Content
	Review Week 1 Content
Week 3 Content	Week 3 Content
	Review Week 2 Content
Week 4 Content	Week 4 Content
	Review Week 1-3 Content
	Test Weeks 1-4 Content
Week 5 Content	Week 5 Content
	Review Week 4 Content

Week 6 Content	Week 6 Content
	Review Week 5 Content
Week 7 Content	Week 7 Content
	Review Weeks 4-6 Content
Week 8 Content	Week 8 Content
Test Weeks 1-8 Content	Review Week 1-6 Content
	Test Weeks 1-6 Content

Question: I barely have time to go through the content once. How will I go through it more than once?

Answer: It's an excellent question and there are good answers. Here are a few ways to have more time to review the most critical content to remember.

- Be sure that need-to-remember content absolutely must be remembered.
- Remove not-needed-now content.
- Remove less-critical content. Offer books and other self-study resources for learning less-critical content.
- Let people read or review less-critical content during less-busy moments.

Question: Should I review critical-to-remember content exactly as I taught it?

Answer: You can. But it often helps to use different strategies such as:

- Teach in presentation mode and repeat in Q&A
- Teach in a lunch-n-learn session and repeat with SMS (text) questions
- Teach in demo mode and repeat in you-do-it (practice) mode
- Teach in asynchronous e-learning and repeat in work-related scenarios with job aids (discussed in Tactic 20)
- Teach in virtual classroom and repeat in work-related scenarios

One reason for using varying approaches is that it can offer different contexts for remembering. Initially, I might not remember what the instructor said, but I might remember the unusual way someone asked a question and the silly way the instructor replied.

One of the reasons flipped learning (usually a blended approach with self-paced lectures and in-class discussion and practice exercises)—with more than one exposure to the concepts—can be ideal.

Spaced remembering

Remembering practice (often called "retrieval practice" in the science of learning literature) means planned opportunities to *practice* remembering. Spaced remembering means purposely increasing planned opportunities to practice remembering. This helps people remember for longer and longer periods of time.

The best way to help people remember what they need to remember is to have them *practice* remembering. How can we make remembering like their on-the-job activities? The obvious answer is real-life practice. But that's not the only way. Here are some others:
- "How would you" questions
- Scenarios
- Case studies
- Action plans

For example, in customer service training, customer service reps may practice remembering which departments handle different types of claims and how to transfer calls to departments in the same building and departments in other locations. In a data safety course, participants may practice remembering the methods for selecting secure passwords, using their chosen secure passwords, and changing passwords.

The combination of repeated learning and repeated remembering cycles may or may not look like 1 or 2 in Figure 7.7. But we want people to have repeated access to the content and the remembering practice.

Figure 7.7 Practical ways of combining spaced learning and spaced remembering

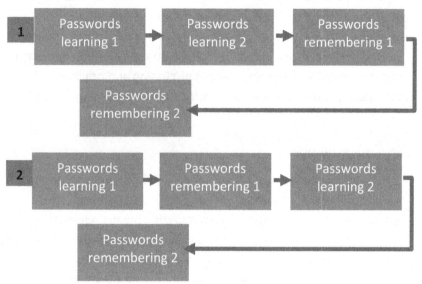

Like spaced learning, research shows that spaced remembering over increasingly long periods helps us remember information over increasingly longer periods of time. As we increase the intervals over time, we help people remember for longer periods of time.

We are always practicing retrieving things from our memory. And, if you think about it, it becomes obvious that the more often you retrieve something, the easier it becomes for you to remember it. For example, if you drive somewhere every two weeks, you will soon be able to remember how to get there without your GPS. If you prefer a certain type of vanilla extract but only buy it every four months, you may have to look up the brand on your Amazon orders list.

Question: How far apart should I space remembering sessions?

Answer: Spaced practice often works best if, over time, we increase the interval between practice sessions. We might start at one day, then two days, then three days, then five days, then a week, then 10 days, then two weeks, and so on.

For example, if people need to use information about every three weeks to a month, work up to one-month intervals.

How can you space learning and remembering in your projects?

Resource: Spaced Learning, Spaced Remembering

There are many good resources on spaced learning and spaced practice, if you want to get deeper into the weeds.

My colleague, Dr. Will Thalheimer, writes terrific reports about learning research. He has a report called *Spacing Learning Over Time*. It's perfect if you want a much deeper dive on this topic—and I am telling you about it with his permission.

http://www.willatworklearning.com/2014/06/spacing-learning-over-time-research-report.html

Tactic 19: Support Memory with Memory Aids

In Tactic 18 I discussed spacing both learning and remembering activities to improve what people can remember from instruction. We can also help memory in the here-and-now by building physical or digital memory aids (and helping people use them). They are typically called job aids, but they are also known as cheat sheets, checklists, and other names.

Job aids help people perform *now*. They supply summaries of needed information and help people avoid mistakes or remind them what to do. They can be physical or digital.

In *Writing and Organizing for Deeper Learning*, Tactic 26 discusses making certain types of instructional content job ready. That is what I will discuss here, but the focus here is how to assist (limited working) memory rather than what kinds of content to build.

Table 7.2 shows typical types of job aids and an example of each type we might use to help employees with business travel. Figure 7.8 shows a partial example of a procedure job aid for filing your expense report after business travel.

Table 7.2 Typical job aid types and examples for business travel

Job aid type	Example job aid
Checklist: Items to consider or do	Travel checklist
Procedure: The steps to perform	How to file your travel expense report
Decision guides: Tables or flowcharts with criteria that guide choices	When you can use alternate airlines and hotels
Reference: Collections of information	Hotel and airline codes

Figure 7.8 Partial example of a procedure job aid for filing an expense report

File Your Expense Report

NOTE: You have 14 calendar days starting the day you return from business travel to submit your expense report.

1. Gather *paper and electronic receipts* for your expenses. You will attach electronic receipts to your expense report. Send paper receipts to HR306 in interoffice mail in Step 7.

2. Log into the *Staff Self-Service Portal*. Then click on the *Travel* folder.

3. You see a list of your recent trips, with the *most recent* at the top. Click on the trip for which you wish to create a travel expense report.

4. Enter the codes for airlines, hotels, car rentals...   Airline codes
Hotel codes
Car rental codes

Question: Can't people just go back to the learning module and look up what they need? Why develop separate job aids?
Answer: Many people don't read manuals that come with the appliances or the tech products they buy. They are not going to dig through a training module to find the information they are seeking. Plus, the information may not be in the best format for use on the job. If we are interested in helping them remember, it's our responsibility to make it usable.

We can build many types of physical and electronic job aids that help people on the job. Job aids can also help people remember without the use of the job aid over time. The best times to use a job aid:

- After learning, to remember what to do
- When there are changes, to remember what has changed
- When tasks are infrequent, to remember the steps

And some of the best reasons for using job aids are:
- To reduce time to proficiency
- To reduce errors
- To understand needed outcomes of steps or tasks
- For more consistent performance

Many times, we can take content we developed for training and repurpose it as job aids people can use on the job without having to dig through the training (because most won't). For example, a medical systems training group built training for a medical information system. As part of the training, they built a series of short how-to videos and job aids. To get workers used to using the job aids, they had people download the job aid to use during the training (Figure 7.9).

Figure 7.9 Job aids used during system training

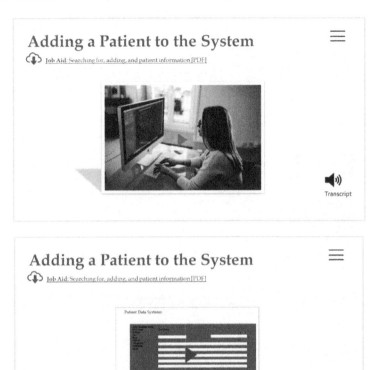

After training, the videos and job aids from the systems training (Figure 7.10) were available in one location.

Figure 7.10 Videos and job aids from the training for use as post-training memory aids

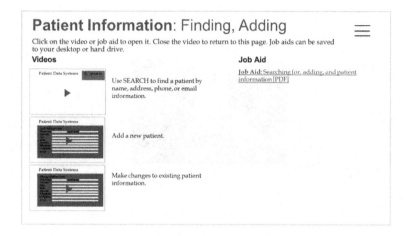

How can you use memory aids in your projects?

 Resource: Job Aids

Writing job aids is a skill. They need to be concise and clear and, for that reason, I recommend starting with my *Write and Organize for Deeper Learning* book. But that book is general, so I also recommend a few job aid-specific resources.

My friend Dave Ferguson has a collection of job aid examples listed by type. He's an excellent and humorous writer and his job aid collection is available from the URL in Figure 7.11. You can learn a lot from reviewing and analyzing his examples.

Figure 7.11 Dave Ferguson's Ensampler (http://www.ensampler.com).

Allison Rosset is a well-known authority and writer in our industry. Her books *Job Aids and Performance Support: Moving from Knowledge in the Classroom to Knowledge Everywhere* and *A Handbook of Job Aids* provide good advice on writing and using job aids. Atul Gawande's book, *The Checklist Manifesto*, explains how simple checklists can prevent mistakes and problems in many fields. I recommend it highly.

Tactic 20: Support Essential Skill Upkeep

When we use knowledge rarely, we often find the knowledge harder to recall. For example, before we had digital systems for friends' and colleagues' phone numbers (such as the contacts app on our smart phone), people remembered many people's phone numbers. Now? We look them up.

When we use a skill rarely, the skill decays. My first computers were Macs. But I switched to Windows-based computers to use instructional development apps that ran primarily on Windows. Recently, when borrowing someone's Mac, I was sad to realize I didn't remember how to use it.

For critical knowledge and skills we recall or use rarely (but want to be able to recall or use), we must find ways to keep the knowledge recallable and the skills usable. But how? Tactics 18 and 19 offer good options. We can space learning and repetitions of very critical information so it doesn't become easily forgotten. And we can offer memory aids to remind people of what to do.

But what about knowledge and skills we must use quickly and easily or automatically, despite not having chances to regularly remember or use them on the job? I show an enlarged version of the right side of the remembering continuum (Tactic 2, Figure 4.5).

Figure 7.12 Right side of remembering continuum

Skills we remember quickly and easily   **Automated skills**

Making knowledge and skills available quickly and easily or automatically requires regular practice. For instance, some people may fill in for others on certain work tasks as needed. But filling in doesn't work well unless the people filling in can perform the tasks.

This became perfectly obvious to me during a winter ice storm when I was the only person who made it to my work location. Although I managed the location, I didn't know how to make health education appointments or take reservations for the conference center. Maybe I didn't need to know how. But it became clear that day that I should have thought through whether I needed to be trained and remain skilled.

Research on automating behavior shows it has plusses and minuses. Automatic processes use minimal attention capacity and are therefore very efficient. We rarely think about how to drive while driving to work—we just get there. Our brain wants to automate as much as possible to make life easier and save attentional processes for more critical issues. Imagine having to plan and think through every step: fixing breakfast, brushing your teeth, driving to work, and so forth. Agony!

But a lack of awareness can cause problems. We do not notice how we see the same ways and our recurring biases, laziness, and default processes. We also tend to take shortcuts, which is why checklists and other job aids can reduce error.

When we train people to do things automatically (or, over time, certain behaviors become automatic) we must be sure the knowledge and skills are correct because automated skills are automatic and not thought through.

When deciding to train so people can do skills easily or automatically, we should:
1. Determine what skills are critical enough to be automated.
2. Determine the guidelines and outcomes needed.
3. Build a practice schedule for skills not performed regularly.
4. Update guidelines and outcomes as needed.
5. Update 1-4 as needed.

Figure 7.13 shows a partial example of a skills proficiency log used to document practice of skills that are not used often.

Figure 7.13 Critical Care Proficiency Log

Task	Proficiency	Date Checked
Arterial Lines	Guidelines	1/17, 5/22
EKG	Guidelines	1/17, 4/10
Nasogastric Tube	Guidelines	2/12
Pulmonary Artery Catheter	Guidelines	2/12, 4/10
Tracheostomy	Guidelines	3/01, 5/22
Ventilator	Guidelines	2/12, 5/22

Try It

We have reached the end of the tactics for **Strategy 4: Practice for Remembering.** Select instruction you want—or someone has asked you—to build. Then use the tactics in this chapter (recapped below) to add practice elements that improve remembering.

Tactic 16	Use Real Context(s) Embed your audience's actual job context during instruction. This helps people remember when they're back on the job.
Tactic 17	Use Self-explanations Have participants put main concepts in their own words and explain the importance of the concept to their own work.
Tactic 18	Space Learning and Remembering To increase remembering: Repeat main points over time. Repetition can be in different formats. Then practice remembering over increasing intervals to help people remember over longer time intervals.
Tactic 19	Support Memory with Memory Aids Build physical or digital job aids (such as checklists, procedure steps, and decision guides) to help people remember what they need to remember in the moment and reduce errors.
Tactic 20	Support Essential Skill Upkeep Eliminate or reduce critical knowledge or skill decay by setting up practice times to keep these items fresh.

Consider doing this exercise with a group of people so you can discuss the following with others:
- What was helpful, less helpful?
- What did you learn?
- Which parts of this exercise will you continue to use in the future?

CHAPTER 8

Strategy 5: Give Effective Feedback

Research shows that feedback's mechanisms during instruction are complex and often misunderstood. *Effective* feedback positively affects learning outcomes and motivation to learn and can help build accurate schema. But other types of feedback can demotivate and reduce learning.

In the tactics ahead, I'll discuss what types of feedback to give, when to give it, and how to structure it. Because feedback is complex, if you didn't read Chapter 3, Why Practice and Feedback, you may want to read it before reading this chapter. It sets the stage for why practice and feedback are two sides of the same coin and why neither is as effective without the other. Figure 8.1 lists the tactics for this chapter.

Figure 8.1 Feedback tactics that help people know how they are doing and how they need to improve

Tactic 21: Keep the Focus on Learning
Tactic 22: Tie Feedback to the Learning Objectives
Tactic 23: Offer the Right Level of Information
Tactic 24: Fix Misconceptions
Tactic 25: Give Feedback at the Right Time
Tactic 26: Structure Feedback for Ease of Use

Tactic 21: Keep the Focus on Learning

Can I share a secret with you? Writing this chapter of the book took almost five weeks. Five weeks! I felt frustrated, miserable and, at some points, I thought I wouldn't be able to get it right. Feedback is an extremely complex issue and, although I knew a lot about it, after I read and re-read the primary research I found it hard to decide which issues to include and exclude.

I promised to write these books in a way you could read and apply. But the issue of feedback didn't seem to lend itself to this format. I could have changed the title of the book from *Practice and Feedback for Deeper Learning* to just *Practice for Deeper Learning*. But practice and feedback go together.

I finally relied on Marie Forleo's phrase, "Everything is figureoutable." Marie Forleo (www.marieforleo.com) is the owner of MarieTV, builds entrepreneur training programs I have used, and is an all-round great person. I just kept moving forward (and sometimes backward) and told myself that the format and answers would reveal themselves in time.

Why did I tell you this story? To make a point: The focus of formative (in-progress) feedback is *learning*. We *expect* people who are learning to falter, fall, have misunderstandings, need help, and all the things that go along with learning. If they didn't need to learn, they wouldn't need our help.

If we are facilitating learning, we need them to know we have their back. This may sound like philosophy but research backs it. When writing this book, I was learning how to make incredibly complex subjects far less complex. Once I took off the pressure to perform and allowed it to be a learning experience, I worked my way through it.

To focus on learning we can

- Offer clear, job-focused learning objectives, including criteria

- Show people what the learning objectives involve using examples, models, and other exemplars
- Help people see the progress they are making toward the learning objectives as well as areas needing improvement

Tactic 22: Tie Feedback to the Learning Objectives

Feedback is most valuable when it communicates the specific gap between current knowledge and skill and targeted knowledge and skill *by specifying how to meet the target*. In instruction, the targeted knowledge and skill are the learning objectives. This is called "formative feedback," as its purpose is to inform follow-up actions and learning. The full benefits of feedback occur only if the feedback directs further practice.

Tactic 10 tells us to tie practice directly to the learning objectives. To make feedback specific and meaningful, it should address precise aspects of work we address through the learning objectives—not generalities or personality issues.

Feedback should specifically target how to move forward toward the learning objectives.

For example, we know that one of the main causes of falls in construction accidents is not adhering to the three-points-of-contact rule, whereby a worker using a ladder keeps three points of contact with the ladder always. This usually means two feet and one hand are always in contact with the ladder. Three points of contact prevents body positions that are less stable and more likely to result in falls.

Figure 8.2 shows the objectives shown to participants of a ladder safety course for construction workers (from Figure 4.7).

Figure 8.2 Learning objectives for the ladder safety course

To reduce the risk to life and limb from construction ladder falls, you will:
1. Decide which ladder or other apparatus to use in a specific work situation
2. Inspect the ladder before use
3. Position a ladder safely
4. Use the ladder safely
5. Make a hazardous situation safe
6. Help others protect their health and safety

Objective 4 has four sub-objectives:
    4.1 Do not stand on the top two steps of a stepladder—or the top four steps of an extension ladder.
    4.2 Always keep three points of contact with the ladder while working on it.
    4.3 Don't carry anything while climbing a ladder.
    4.4 Have someone else hold the ladder while you climb to your destination.

Figure 8.3 shows a question from the ladder safety course related to learning objective 4.

Figure 8.3 Question from ladder safety course

Figure 8.4 shows two potential feedback answers. Which feedback answer do you think is more job-specific? Please decide which answer is more job-specific and why you think so before continuing. The answer is below Figure 8.4, but you will learn more by thinking through this issue than jumping right to the answer!

Figure 8.4 Possible feedback options

Feedback 1	**Feedback 2**
Question: Can Elena safely work from the top of the ladder on the insulation?	*Question:* Can Elena safely work from the top of the ladder on the insulation?
The correct answer is .	The correct answer is .
It is not safe for Elena to work on the top of the ladder because she cannot keep **three points of contact** at the top.	Elena cannot work safely from the top of the ladder because standing at the top of the ladder places her at increased risk for falling.
Three points of contact means keeping two feet and one hand in contact with the ladder.	

> Patti's answer:
>
> The more specific and task-related feedback is feedback 1 because it offers a reminder about the three-points-of-contact rule people should use to prevent falls.
>
> The participant did not accurately retrieve this information from memory during the activity so we will likely want to ask another question (Figure 8.5) to make sure they can retrieve this information correctly.

Figure 8.5 Possible follow-up questions

Use the ladder safely

Three-points-of-contact helps you stay safer on a stepladder because:

A. You are required to tie the top and the bottom of the ladder to fixed points.
B. It reduces steeper angles, which are more likely to cause falls.
C. It reduces body positions where you are more likely to fall.

Click the *best* answer.

The correct answer is .

This is because three points of contact with a ladder, such as two feet and one hand, keeps your body close to the ladder. It avoids outstretched body positions where it is easier to lose your balance.

Tie feedback to job-specific learning objectives.

Tactic 23: Offer the Right Level of Information

We can offer several types of information for feedback. Table 8.1 shows a progression of increasingly detailed feedback, from knowledge of results to helping people understand what error(s) they made to telling them how to correct the error. There are even more types of feedback (really?) but I narrowed it down to the types most often used in learning in organizations.

Table 8.1 Amount of feedback

	Level	Description
less ↑	Knowledge of Results (KR)	Correctness of response *Example*: Your answer is correct.
	Knowledge of Correct Results (KCR)	The correct answer *Example:* The correct answer *is clean paper towels.*
	Help	Hints Examples Help finding error *Example:* **What else can contaminate...?**
	Error(s)	Type of error(s), such as Missing or incorrect knowledge, associations, or skills Mistakes Misconceptions *Example:* **It is commonly misunderstood that any towel will work, but...**
↓ *more*	Correction(s)	How to correct *Example:* **Put clean paper towels next to the hand-washing sink...**

Research is a bit confusing but, in general, it shows that people learn better from feedback that tells them the correct response and explains why. People with less knowledge about the topic tend to want to confirm that their answers are correct—and almost everyone wants to know why their wrong answers are wrong.

Figure 8.6 shows an activity from a data security course and the feedback on the activity.

Figure 8.6 Two-factor authentication activity (top) and feedback (bottom)

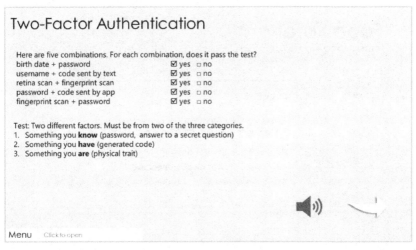

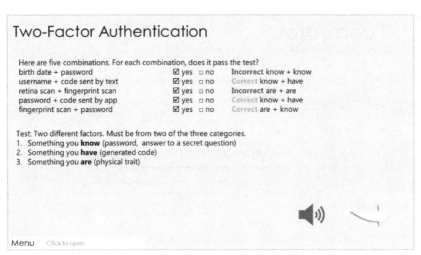

Figure 8.7 shows two versions of feedback from a food safety course. The top version is very specific and the bottom version adds even more information. Which do you think is better? Please decide

which answer is better and why you think so before continuing. The answer is on the next page, but you will learn more by thinking through this issue than jumping right to the answer!

Figure 8.7 Two versions of feedback: less information (top) and more information (bottom)

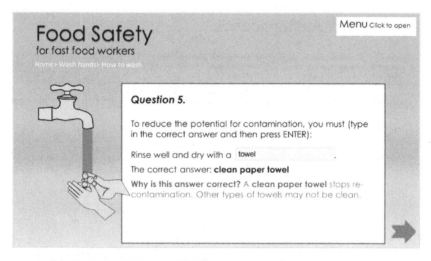

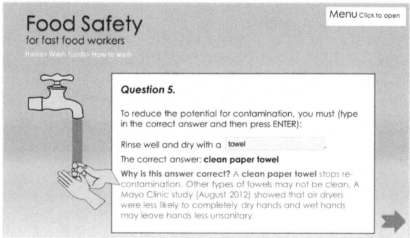

Patti's answer:

The better feedback is the top version because it supplies the correct answer and why—and nothing else. We weren't talking about hand dryers, so this adds confusing information that takes away from the most critical information to remember.

Always consider the information people need at this point in their learning journey. The newer they are to the topic, the more likely you should give only enough feedback to correct the specific mistake or misconception.

Confirm the right answer and why it is correct.

Tactic 24: Fix Misconceptions

One of the largest problems during instruction is misconception—some people simply accept what they are learning, as we discussed about surface learning in Chapter 2. But deep learning, or learning for application, requires understanding. When we misunderstand something, we either must find a way to fit what we are learning around this misconception, or move forward without understanding what we are learning.

Consider one idea people often misunderstand when dealing with money: *the time value of money*. The time value of money tells us that a certain amount of money received today has greater value than the same amount of money received in the future. Example: You have the option of receiving $1,000 today or $1,000 in five years. The first option is more valuable because:

1. **Risk:** Having the money now eliminates the risk of waiting.
2. **Value:** Because of the likelihood of inflation, $1,000 today is likely worth more than $1,000 in five years.
3. **Opportunity cost:** Money received today can earn interest, creating more money. Money received in the future can't earn interest today.

When we want to compare money now and in the future, we use the time-value-of-money concept and two procedures (that we can do using Excel® or other financial calculators): compounding and discounting. Most people make the mistake of simply comparing the two amounts—not realizing money has different values at different times. For example, if a relative borrows $10,000 and will pay you back in five years, the $10,000 they give you is worth less than the $10,000 you gave them because of discounting.

Misconceptions are known to be extremely damaging to learning. We are not teaching people who are blank slates. Adults typically have prior knowledge of the topic or related knowledge. One of the first things we try to do, when learning, is relate what we are learning to what we know.

Prior or related knowledge can be accurate, but it can also be inaccurate and have missing pieces. Misconceptions are common. They can be wrong or partially wrong for many reasons. Sometimes prior knowledge is inaccurate and makes it hard to accurately learn new information. People also bring preconceptions and beliefs, which can be difficult to change.

Deeper learning requires that we find and fix misconceptions—especially things people know that are inaccurate—as they damage future understanding and application. This is one of the most critical tasks for feedback.

Find misconceptions

In Strategy 1: Analyze the Job Content, Tactic 5: Find the Typical Misconceptions, we find the typical mistakes people make and the typical misconceptions people have. You will use these issues in developing practice and feedback.

There are many methods we can use to find out what people know that may be inaccurate, partially inaccurate, or misguided. Table 8.2 offers three ways to figure out what misconceptions and preconceptions people have and insights about what not to assume.

Table 8.2 Methods for finding misconceptions and how to not assume people understand

Try these methods	But don't...
Ask "why" and "how" questions and ask how concepts are related.	Assume relationships are obvious and everyone understands.
Ask people what they already know about the topic. An open discussion allows us to openly gauge the level of understanding and preconceptions.	Think there is only one, obvious way to interpret the content. People who have different prior knowledge and preconceptions WILL interpret it differently.

Discuss situations and examples to gauge understanding and preconceptions.	Assume people understood your content, activity, or demonstration the way you intended.
Use questions, with common misunderstandings as distractors (incorrect answers). Show the correct answer and then offer evidence for the correct answer.	Assume what is clear to you will be clear to others. Verify.

    I regularly use the methods in Table 8.2 in workshops and conference presentations. I especially like the last method for conference presentations on the learning sciences because it brings about extremely lively discussion. For example, I know from experience that the issue of "learning styles"—a concept that refers to people having preferential styles of how they like to learn—is a hot topic. But the learning sciences have debunked the topic, saying we may *prefer* certain things but research shows that these preferences do not affect learning. What affects learning the most is following the research.

    As an example of using the last technique, Figure 8.8 shows three of the slides I regularly use to discuss the use of research-based tactics in learning.

Figure 8.8 Three slides about "learning styles" misconceptions from *Write and Organize* slide deck

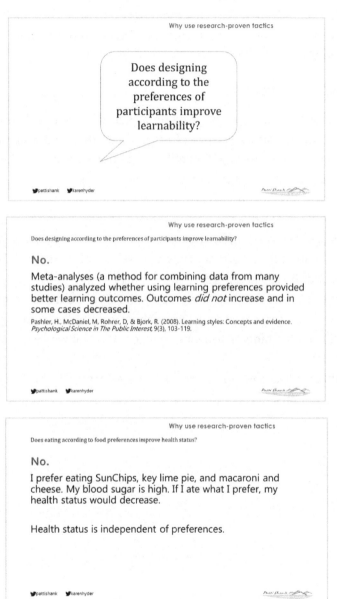

As I discussed in Chapter 3, it isn't helpful and may be harmful to give discouraging feedback. When people tell me they still think learning styles have merit, I tell them to get in touch with me if they want to read the actual research. I can also be skeptical and often need to see for myself.

Fix misconceptions

Because misconceptions often derail learning, we should use the best methods learning science offers to repair them. Although we may think simply offering the right information to people should fix misconceptions, research shows this is not the case. And it also shows that misconceptions can be very sticky.

For example, airplanes stay aloft using aerodynamic lift, but numerous textbooks, encyclopedias, and even flight manuals provide an explanation that is wrong. They discuss "equal transit time" of the air around the top and bottom of the wings as the reason for lift. But airplanes fly because their wings cause the air pressure underneath to be greater than that above, lifting them into the air. Although the scientific understanding has long changed, the faulty explanation is still in use.

Table 8.3 lists some of the most powerful methods for fixing misconceptions.

Table 8.3 Methods to fix misconceptions

Methods	Discussion
Prevention	Use quizzing, questions, and similar methods to prevent misconceptions from starting, whenever possible. Because of prior knowledge and preconceptions, this is not always easy to do. But we should prevent misconceptions from forming whenever possible.
Metacognition (See Strategy 2)	Help people become aware of their own preconceptions and how these preconceptions impact learning.
Self-explanations (see Strategy 4, Tactic 18)	Michelene Chi, Professor of Science and Teaching at Arizona State University, tells us that self-explanations can help people change their mental concepts. This involves having people explain, in their own words, what they are learning—and making connections between related concepts.
Powerful, diverse examples	Use a few diverse and powerful examples that show the problems with multiple misconceptions, rather than many examples that show the problems with one. This method is more powerful and easier to remember.
Case studies and situations	Use case studies and situations to help people analyze the validity of their current-versus-possible knowledge side-by-side.
Strengthening	If we help people overcome misconceptions, have them strengthen correct knowledge with application in real-life situations.

Find and fix misconceptions so people can continue to learn.

Tactic 25: Give Feedback at the Right Time

The timing of feedback relates to how soon we give it after an answer or performance. Like a lot of feedback insights, there aren't fixed rules about when to offer feedback. The main insight for timing feedback is to offer it *when it will be most beneficial*. And the most beneficial time is when you can put the feedback into practice.

The best time to offer feedback is when people can *use* the feedback information.

For example, when you learned to ride a bike, if you received feedback ("Pedal faster!") at the *end* of each bike-riding session, you would likely forget it before the next session. If you received a lot of feedback at the end of every two or three bike riding sessions ("Try to build up speed quickly. Keep your body upright. Pedal faster. Don't look down or back at me. Relax your arms a bit.") you'd be overwhelmed. And you'd likely forget all the advice before the next bike-riding session.

Hattie's research shows that regular, valuable feedback helps people stay on track toward learning goals. And regular, valuable feedback keeps misconceptions from getting fixed in memory to derail further learning.

Feedback is *most valuable right before people are about to apply it*. When is that? Table 9.4 lists three instructional activities, suggested feedback for each activity, and two possible times for offering the feedback. For each activity, which time do you think is better? Please decide which answer is better and why you think so before continuing. The answer is below, but you will learn more by thinking through this issue than jumping right to the answer!

Table 8.4 Best time for feedback

Activity	Feedback	Best time?
1. Write the first draft of a persuasive email	Feedback on content and tone of email	A. Before writing the second draft B. At the end of the lesson on writing a persuasive email
2. Select the performance review that is most legally defensible	Which answer is correct and why is it correct?	A. Before selecting the next legally defensible performance review B. At the end of the lesson on writing a legally defensible performance review
3. Drunk driving scenario	Consequences of driving after two beers	A. While driving home B. At home

> Patti's answer:
>
> The better feedback timing is the top one in each situation **because it offers the feedback right before there is a need to apply the feedback. In activity 3, if the person makes it home, he or she has no opportunity to apply the feedback. In scenarios 1 and 2, the feedback could still be applied in the B answer but the recipient may have forgotten the feedback at this point.

Delayed feedback can be helpful if people *are able* to find and fix their own mistakes. As I discussed in Strategy 2: Practice for Self-Sufficiency, helping workers become self-sufficient at learning is very useful as a life skill.

Offer feedback WHEN people can apply it.

When people do not have much prior knowledge in the topic or domain—or are uncertain—they are often unable to self-correct. The best hints at this point are helping people see the hidden rules or strategies embedded in the topic. For example, when teaching people how to fix errors with building a table of contents in Microsoft Word, the strategy is to run the table of contents, look for errors, and then look at the styles applied to those errors.

When training people to fix errors in their table of contents, rather than tell them how to fix each error, I could ask people to run the table of contents and look for any:

- Headings that are missing: Check the heading to see if the right heading style was applied.
- Headings are at the wrong heading level: Check the heading to see if the right heading style was applied.
- Non-headings show up as a heading: Check the heading to see if the right heading style was applied.

After this activity, I would ask the following question: *How can we fix most problems we find in the table of contents?*

When we help people self-correct, we offer specific hints and help messages. For example, the two-factor authentication activity (Figure 8.9) shows what people need to do at the bottom of the activity.

Figure 8.9 Guidance for the activity below the question

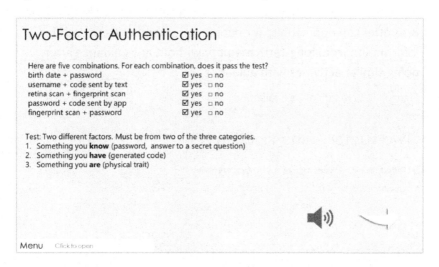

Figure 8.10 shows a choice for getting guidance by clicking on the button. It doesn't provide the answers, but help is there if anyone wants to use it.

Figure 8.10 Guidance available for the activity

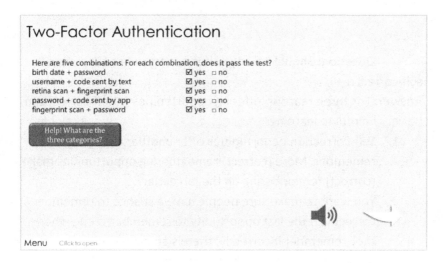

Because we offered help in earlier activities, we may want to make sure people can do what they need to do without help. Figure 8.11 offers an opportunity for people to remember (retrieve) this information from long-term memory without any guidance after doing similar activities with guidance.

Figure 8.11 No guidance available

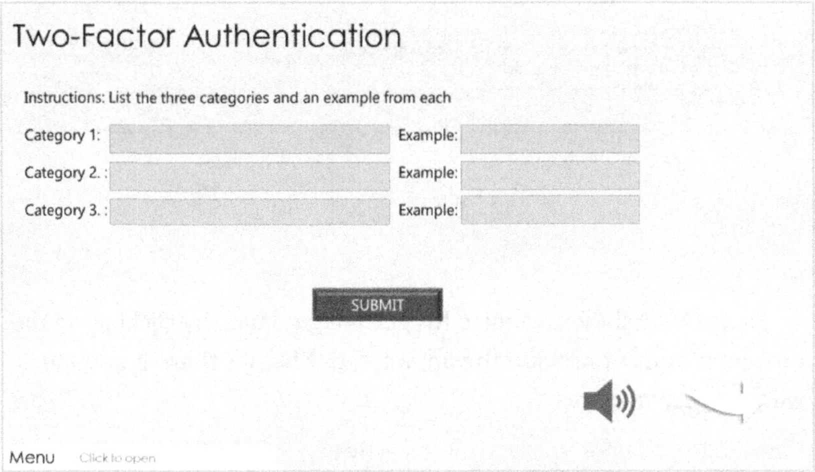

Two-Factor Authentication

Instructions: List the three categories and an example from each

Category 1: _____   Example: _____
Category 2: _____   Example: _____
Category 3: _____   Example: _____

SUBMIT

Menu   Click to open

Question: Should I always offer opportunities for people to self-correct?

Answer: For three reasons, offering opportunities to self-correct can be very helpful to learning:

1. Self-correction opportunities offer another chance to remember. More (correct) remembering opportunities make (correct) remembering on the job easier.
2. You want to make sure people have a chance to remember correctly. If the last opportunity to remember is one where they remember incorrectly, there's an increased chance they will continue to remember incorrectly.

3. Self-correction teaches people they should try to self-correct. This is an important life skill.

There are many options for self-correction practice during instruction. Here are a few of my favorites:
- Ask questions:
    - Where did we talk about this?
    - What were the most important points?
    - How did you decide which answer is correct?
    - How confident are you that this is the correct answer? Why?
- Collaboration: Discuss your answer with someone else. Did you arrive at the same answer? Why do you think your answers are the same or different?

Self-correction opportunities are powerful. But they can also be mentally challenging. Use them when people can handle them and you want to build self-sufficiency.

Tactic 26: Structure Feedback for Ease of Use

If we offer feedback at the wrong time, it may not be applied—or it may be forgotten. If feedback is disorganized, it may be too difficult to apply. To manage cognitive load when offering feedback (especially complex feedback), we should offer feedback in sequence and categorized by the factors being evaluated. Remember the relationship of work performance to learning objectives and practice and feedback? Work performance gives us the needed learning objectives. Those learning objectives tell us what practice is needed and how to evaluate it (feedback).

We'll reuse the example of training people to build a table of contents using Microsoft Word Heading Styles. We can organize feedback according to the learning objectives for the final practice activity: Build your own document with a table of contents. I show how the feedback is organized (by learning objective) in Figure 8.12.

Figure 8.12 Feedback for each learning objective

Don't use a TOC when there are fewer than five pages.
Your document has 12 pages. Using a table of contents follows company guidelines.

Create heading styles using Microsoft Word heading styles.
You created the table of contents using MS Word heading styles.

Use parallel wording in your headings when possible.
Most of the items are parallel. In the fourth heading, Compare Before and After, two of the subheadings use "ing" while two don't. You should make them all the same.

Make sure headings are understandable to readers.
Will all your readers understand the technical terms? If not, use more familiar terms.

Add the table of contents to your document after the cover and before the introduction.
The table of contents is in the right place.

The main point is that feedback should be organized rather than a mishmash or jumble of words. For example, when offering feedback on a single practice exercise, how will you write it? I show two possibilities of an organized approach below. (I like B better because people may forget how they answered.)

A	B
The correct answer is [].	You answered [].
The reason [] is correct is	The correct answer is [].
	The reason [] is correct is

Question: In our online learning programs, we only give feedback (correct/incorrect, the reason why for each question, and % of questions correct) at the end of the program. It seems to me—from everything written in this section—that this isn't a good plan. Am I right?

Answer: What you are describing is summative feedback—and it's a different kind of feedback. I specifically concentrated on formative evaluation (the type that helps people learn and reach the learning objectives) in this chapter rather than summative evaluation because it's what works best with practice.

The goal of summative feedback is performance assessment. Although that may be a final goal, if we push for performance and assessment before we have helped people achieve mastery, we can make it more difficult to learn. There's absolutely nothing wrong with summative assessment, but our first goal is to help people learn. I believe we often give it too little emphasis.

Try It

We have reached the end of the tactics for **Strategy 5: Give Effective Feedback.** Select instruction you want—or someone has asked you—to build. Then use the tactics in this chapter (recapped below) to add effective feedback or plan for effective feedback.

Tactic 21	**Keep the Focus on Learning** Reduce the anxiety in learning by offering the right attitude, support, examples, tools, and other materials. We are not here to only build content.
Tactic 22	**Tie Feedback to the Learning Objectives** Feedback should communicate the gap between the learning objective and current knowledge and skills. The goal of feedback is to inform next steps in the learning process.
Tactic 23	**Offer the Right Level of Information** Determine what information people need at their place in their learning journey—and give them that information. People with less prior knowledge generally do best with the correct answer and why it's correct.
Tactic 24	**Fix Misconceptions** Deep learning requires understanding. Misunderstandings (misconceptions) damage what people know—and often damage further learning. We need to find and fix them.
Tactic 25	**Give Feedback at the Right Time** Timing of feedback is important. Typically, the best time for feedback is when people can put the feedback information into practice.
Tactic 26	**Structure Feedback for Ease of Use** If feedback is hard to use, it likely won't be used.

Consider doing this exercise with a group of people so you can discuss the following with others:
- What was helpful, less helpful?
- What did you learn?
- Which parts of this exercise will you continue to use in the future?

CHAPTER 9

Now What?

This chapter contains four tools to help you use the strategies and tactics in this book.

1. A **remembering practice activity** to help you remember the strategies and tactics in this book. It will be easier for you to use the tactics if you don't have to continually refer to the book.
2. A **checklist** (job aid) that lists all the strategies and tactics in the book—and a few notes to help you remember them. It's hard (but not impossible, especially if you use the retrieval practice activity) to remember 26 tactics, but the checklist will help you. Feel free to annotate them with your own notes and insights from the book.
3. A list of **references**—the research articles and books that support the strategies and tactics. I don't expect you to read them, but I want you to have them in case you want to read them.

I'd be grateful if you could tell me what you think of this book. Was the book valuable to you? Why or why not? Was it worth what you paid? What would you change? What other topics would you like me to write about in this series? Here are some of the topics I'm considering writing about next:

- Assessments for Deeper Learning
- Questions and Examples for Deeper Learning
- Analyzing Performance and Building Simple Solutions
- Building Simple Performance Support

You can reach out by emailing me at patti@pattishank.com. Use a descriptive subject line (such as: Comments on your Practice and Feedback book) so I am sure to open your email!

I use what you tell me to revise and fine-tune what I write—and get super excited when readers write to me. It often makes my day! And I'm especially grateful there are other learning geeks who want to make a real difference in their organizations and elsewhere. Yay!!!

Thank YOU.

Retrieval Practice

Retrieval practice is a powerful learning activity for improving recall of specific information. Try to list the tactics without looking through the book. Check your answers against the table of contents or the checklist that follows. Then correct your answers and practice memorizing the right answers for five minutes. Try again in a few days. Keep doing this at slightly longer intervals.

Date: Try 1

Strategies	What are the tactics for each strategy?
Strategy 1: Analyze the Job Context (Tactics 1–7)	
Strategy 2: Practice for Self-direction (Tactics 8–9)	

Strategy 3: Practice for Transfer (Tactics 10–15)

Strategy 4: Practice for Remembering (Tactics 16–20)

Strategy 5: Give Effective Feedback (Tactics 21–26)

How many did you get right?   /26

Date: Try 2

Strategies	What are the tactics for each strategy?
Strategy 1: Analyze the Job Context (Tactics 1–7)	
Strategy 2: Practice for Self-direction (Tactics 8–9)	
Strategy 3: Practice for Transfer (Tactics 10–15)	

Strategy 4: Practice
for Remembering
(Tactics 16–20)

Strategy 5: Give
Effective Feedback
(Tactics 21–26)

How many did you get right?   /26

Date: Try 3

Strategies	What are the tactics for each strategy?
Strategy 1: Analyze the Job Context (Tactics 1–7)	
Strategy 2: Practice for Self-direction (Tactics 8–9)	
Strategy 3: Practice for Transfer (Tactics 10–15)	

Strategy 4: Practice
for Remembering
(Tactics 16–20)

Strategy 5: Give
Effective Feedback
(Tactics 21–26)

How many did you get right?   /26

Date: Try 4

Strategies	What are the tactics for each strategy?
Strategy 1: Analyze the Job Context (Tactics 1–7)	
Strategy 2: Practice for Self-direction (Tactics 8–9)	
Strategy 3: Practice for Transfer (Tactics 10–15)	

Strategy 4: Practice for Remembering (Tactics 16–20)	
Strategy 5: Give Effective Feedback (Tactics 21–26)	

How many did you get right?   /26

Practice and Feedback for Deeper Learning Checklist

Purpose: Use this job aid/checklist as a memory aid for the strategies and tactics in this book. The descriptions to the right of the tactics are concise recommendations distilled from the book.

Strategy 1: Analyze the Job Context

Tactic 1	**Connect Learning Objectives to Job Tasks** Write learning objectives that reflect what people should DO (current or upcoming job tasks), not topics.
Tactic 2	**Analyze Conditions Under Which People Perform the Tasks** Understand the conditions under which the tasks are performed. Conditions help us understand what people do and how they do it.
Tactic 3	**Evaluate What Must Be Remembered and What Can Be Looked Up** Find out what people need to commit to memory and what they can look up. Where on the remembering continuum is this information?
Tactic 4	**Analyze Social Processes** What are the social learning and social processes needed for optimal work outcomes? Clarify the social processes and skills that make desired outcomes more likely. What processes and skills must be trained?
Tactic 5	**Find the Typical Misconceptions** How may prior knowledge affect how people view what they are learning? What are typical misconceptions people have about what they are learning?
Tactic 6	**Find Out What Gets in the Way** Find out how work environment and individual performance factors affect trained skills. What can we do to fix these issues so good training outcomes are possible?
Tactic 7	**Assess Support for Skills** Find out if there is adequate support for trained skills on the job. If not, find out how to increase support; otherwise, training should be delayed or abandoned.

Strategy 2: Practice for Self-direction

Tactic 8	**Work Toward Specific, Difficult, and Attainable Goals** Develop learning goals that • Are specific and difficult • Have a clear rationale • Are attainable with the provided training • Focus on learning • Offer feedback that helps people know how they are progressing toward goals
Tactic 9	**Use Self-directed Learning Strategies** Use self-directed questions and individual or collaborative strategies to help people and teams plan, monitor, and evaluate their learning. Create learning paths instead of learning events by adding self-directed learning activities.

Strategy 3: Practice for Transfer

Tactic 10	**Make Training Relevant** Make sure to know and embed the specific and important purposes for the challenges of learning, practicing, using feedback to improve, and applying what people learn during training. Relevance = engagement.
Tactic 11	**Build Practice that Mirrors Work** Use environmental cues, fidelity, consequences, variability, and social interactions to make training like work in the ways that count the most. But, to avoid overwhelming people, analyze which ways are most critical.
Tactic 12	**Show the Right *and* Wrong Ways** Error training helps people understand errors, helps prepare for errors, and often improves the perceived relevance of training.
Tactic 13	**Train How to Handle Errors** Training in error handling has been shown to improve transfer.
Tactic 14	**Use Whole-skill Practice** When teaching complex skills, start with simpler whole-skill practice and move toward more complex whole-skill practice. Training skills as constituent skills leaves out the coordination and integration tasks necessary to performing complex skills.
Tactic 15	**Help with Post-training Support** Help supervisors and team leaders support trained skills by building post-training support items useful to support the training objectives long term.

Strategy 4: Practice for Remembering

Tactic 16	**Use Real Context(s)** Embed your audience's actual job context during instruction. This helps people remember when they're back on the job.
Tactic 17	**Use Self-explanations** Have participants put main concepts in their own words and explain the importance of the concept to their own work.
Tactic 18	**Space Learning and Remembering** To increase remembering: Repeat main points over time. Repetition can be in different formats. Then practice remembering over increasing intervals to help people remember over longer time intervals.
Tactic 19	**Support Memory with Memory Aids** Build physical or digital job aids (such as checklists, procedure steps, and decision guides) to help people remember what they need to remember in the moment and reduce errors.
Tactic 20	**Support Essential Skill Upkeep** Eliminate or reduce critical knowledge or skill decay by setting up practice times to keep these items fresh.

Strategy 5: Give Effective Feedback

Tactic 21	**Keep the Focus on Learning** Reduce the anxiety in learning by offering the right attitude, support, examples, tools, and other materials. We are not here to only build content.
Tactic 22	**Tie Feedback to the Learning Objectives** Feedback should communicate the gap between the learning objective and current knowledge and skills. The goal of feedback is to inform next steps in the learning process.
Tactic 23	**Offer the Right Level of Information** Determine what information people need at this place in their learning journey and give them that information. People with less prior knowledge generally do best with the correct answer and why it's correct.
Tactic 24	**Fix Misconceptions** Deep learning requires understanding. Misunderstandings (misconceptions) damage what people know and often damage further learning. We need to find and fix them.
Tactic 25	**Give Feedback at the Right Time** Timing of feedback is important. Typically, the best time for feedback is when people can put the feedback information into practice.
Tactic 26	**Structure Feedback for Ease of Use** If feedback is hard to use, it likely won't be used.

Want More?

The Make It Learnable series shows you how to apply information and usability research, learning research, and writing research to your instructional projects. This is the second book in the series, and more will be ready soon. To know when they are ready, sign up for email on my website (www.pattishank.com), follow me on Twitter (@pattishank), or check Amazon.

If you want to offer Make It Learnable books to a team, I offer excellent quantity discounts. I can train your team, group, or conference, and supply heavily discounted Make It Learnable books when used in my training sessions. Contact me at patti@learningpeaks.com.

Thank you for helping me improve research-based practices in organizational and adult learning. My goal is to make it easier for *anyone* who writes learning content (including content experts, instructional designers, teachers, and instructors) to build learnable instruction. Just. That. Simple.

What Is the Readability of This Book?

The readability score of the text in this book, according to MS Word's Flesch Reading Ease, is 53.8.

Later versions of Microsoft Word (usually under Word Options) include readability statistics based on Flesch Reading Ease. This readability scale uses scores from 0 to 100. The higher the number, the easier the text is to read. I wanted readability to be around 60 because I didn't want readability to be an issue for *anyone*.

The readability of this book is slightly less than *Write and Organize for Deeper Learning*, which I expected. The topics are a bit more difficult. If the readability was too low, I would have used the tactics in *Write and Organize for Deeper Learning* to improve readability.

Readability Statistics	? ×
Counts	
Words	35,518
Characters	188,172
Paragraphs	1,952
Sentences	2,276
Averages	
Sentences per Paragraph	2.5
Words per Sentence	13.3
Characters per Word	5.0
Readability	
Flesch Reading Ease	53.8
Flesch-Kincaid Grade Level	9.0
Passive Sentences	4.3%
	OK

References

This list includes the references that support the insights and recommendations in this book. I categorized the links, but some could easily appear in more than one place. You will likely be able to find many of these references online by searching for the authors' last names and the title of the research paper. If you can't find a paper, they should be available in academic libraries. My favorite places to find used books are half.com and abebooks.com.

Adult Skills, Job Skills

Deming, D.J. (May 2017). The Growing Importance of Social Skills in the Labor Market. Quarterly Journal of Economics. https://scholar.harvard.edu/ddeming/publications/growing-importance-social-skills-labor-market

Lawrence Mishel, L., J. Bivens, E. Gould, and H. Shierholz. 2012. The State of Working America. 12th edition. Economic Policy Institute, November. www.stateofworkingamerica.org.

Levy, F. & Murnane, R. J. (2013). Dancing with robots: Human skills for computerized work. Third Way & NEXT.

OECD Skills Outlook https://www.oecd.org/skills/piaac

U.S. Department of Education, National Center for Education Statistics, 2003 National Assessment of Adult Literacy https://nces.ed.gov/naal

OECD (2016), Skills Matter: Further Results from the Survey of Adult Skills, OECD Publishing, Paris. http://www.oecd-ilibrary.org/education/oecd-skills-studies_23078731

Pew Research Center. (October 6, 2016). The state of American jobs. http://www.pewsocialtrends.org/2016/10/06/the-state-of-american-jobs/

Schiller, B. (March 15, 2016). Welcome to the Post-Work Economy. http://www.realclearpolicy.com/2016/03/15/welcome_to_the_post-work_economy_30185.html.

World Economic Forum. (January 2016). The Future of Jobs: Employment, Skills and Workforce Strategy for The Fourth Industrial Revolution. http://reports.weforum.org/future-of-jobs-2016/

Rotman, D. (June 12, 2013). How technology is destroying jobs. MIT Technology Review.

Behavior Modeling

Taylor, P. J., Russ-Eft, D. F. & Chan, D. W. L. (2005). A meta-analytic review of behavior modeling training, Journal of Applied Psychology, 90, 692–709.

Deep Learning

Beatie, V., Collins, B., & McInnes, B. (1997). Deep and surface learning: A simple or simplistic dichotomy? Accounting Education, 6(1), 1-12.

Bjork, R. A. (1994). Memory and metamemory considerations in the training of human beings. In J. Metcalfe and A. Shimamura (Eds.), Metacognition: Knowing about knowing. pp. 185–205.

Chin, C. & Brown, D. E. (2000). Learning in science: A comparison of deep and surface approaches. Journal of Research in Science Teaching. 37(2), 109-138.

Craik, F. I. M., & Lockhart, R. S. (1972). Levels of processing: A framework for memory research. Journal of Verbal Learning and Verbal behavior, 11, 671-684.

Craik, F.I.M., & Tulving, E. (1975). Depth of processing and the retention of words in episodic memory. Journal of Experimental Psychology: General, 104, 268-294.

Haggis, T. (2003) Constructing Images of Ourselves? A Critical Investigation into "Approaches to Learning" Research in Higher Education. British Educational Research Journal, 29, 1, 89-104.

Hall, M., Ramsay, A. & Raven, J. (2004) Changing the learning environment to promote deep learning approaches in first year accounting students. Accounting Education 13, 489- 505.

Marton, F., & Säljö, R. (1976). On qualitative differences in learning. I. Outcome and process. British Journal of Educational Psychology, 46, 4-11.

Marton, F., & Säljö, R. (1997). Approaches to learning. In F. Marton, D. J. Hounsell, & N. J. Entwistle (Eds.), The Experience of Learning (2nd ed.). Edinburgh: Scottish Academic Press.

Error Training

Heimbeck, D., Freese, M., Sonnentag, S. & Keith, N. (2003). Integrating errors into the training process: The function of error management instructions and the role of goal orientation, Personnel Psychology, 56, 333–61.

Keith, N. & Frese, M. (2005). Self-regulation in error management training: Emotion control and metacognition as mediators of performance effects, Journal of Applied Psychology, 90, 677–91.

Keith, N. & Frese, M. (2008). Effectiveness of error management training: A meta-analysis, Journal of Applied Psychology, 93, 59–69.

Feedback

Cohen, V. B. (1985). A reexamination of feedback in computer-based instruction: Implications for instructional design. Educational Technology, 25(1) p33-37.

Espasa, A., & Meneses, J. (2009). Analysing feedback processes in an online teaching and learning environment: an exploratory study. Higher Education, 59, 277–292.

Hattie, J. & Yates, G. (2014). Using feedback to promote learning. In V. A. Bekasi, C. E. Overs on, & C. M. Hakala (Eds.). Applying science of learning in education: Infusing psychological science into the curriculum. Retrieved from the Society for the Teaching of Psychology website: http://teachpsych.org/ebooks/asle2014/index.php

Hattie, J., & Gan, M. (2011). Instruction based on feedback. In R. Mayer & P. Alexander (Eds.), Handbook of research on learning and instruction, 249-271. New York: Routledge.

Hattie, J. & Timperley, H. (2007). The power of feedback. Review of Educational Research, 77(1), 81-112.

Kulhavy, R. W. (1977). Feedback in written instruction. Review of Educational Research, 47(1), 211–232.

Kulhavy, R. W., & Stock, W. A. (1989). Feedback in written instruction: The place of response certitude. Educational Psychology Review, 1(4), 279–308.

Moreno, R. (2004). Decreasing Cognitive Load for Novice Students: Effects of Explanatory versus Corrective Feedback in Discovery-Based Multimedia. Instructional Science, 32, 99–113.

Mory, E. (2004). Feedback Research Revisited. In Jonassen, D. (Ed.), Handbook of Research on Educational Communications, 745–784. Mahway, NJ: Lawrence Erlbaum Associates Publishers.

Narciss, S. (2008). Feedback strategies for interactive learning tasks. In J.M. Spector, M.D. Merrill, J.J.G. van Merriënboer, & M.P. Driscoll (Eds.), Handbook of Research on Educational Communications and Technology (3rd ed., pp. 125-144). Mahaw, NJ: Lawrence Erlbaum Associates.

Narciss, S. (2012). Feedback strategies. In N. Seel (Ed.), Encyclopedia of the Learning Sciences, Volume F(6), pp. 1289-1293. New York: Springer Science & Business Media

Narciss, S. & Huth, K. (2004). How to design informative tutoring feedback for multi-media learning. In H. M. Niegemann, D. Leutner & R. Brünken (Eds.), Instructional design for multimedia learning, 181-195. Münster: Waxmann.

Narciss, S. (2012). Feedback in instructional contexts. In N. Seel (Ed.), Encyclopedia of the Learning Sciences, Volume F(6), pp. 1285-1289. New York: Springer Science & Business Media.

Nicol, D., & Macfarlane-Dick, D. (2006). Formative assessment and self-regulated learning: a model and seven principles of good feedback practice. Studies in Higher Education, 31, 199–218.

Shute, V. J. (2007). Focus on Formative Feedback Educational Testing Service, Princeton, NJ.

Fidelity

Alexander, A. L., Brunyé, T., Sidman, J., & Weil, S. A. (2005). From gaming to training: a review of studies on fidelity, immersion, presence, and buy-in and their effects on transfer in pc-based simulations and games. DARWARS Training Impact Group.

Jentsch, F. & Bowers, C. A. (1998). Evidence for the validity of PC-based simulations in studying aircrew coordination. International Journal of Aviation Psychology, 8(3), 243-260.

Interaction, Interactivity

Locke, E. A., & Latham, G. P. (2002). Building a practically useful theory of goal setting and task motivation: A 35-year odyssey. American Psychologist, 57(9), 705-717.

Interaction, Interactivity

Anderson, T. (2003a). Getting the mix right again: An updated and theoretical rationale for interaction.
International Review of Research in Open and Distance Learning, 4(2). http://www.irrodl.org/index.php/irrodl/article/view/149/230

Anderson, T. (2003b). Modes of interaction in distance education: Recent developments and research questions. In D. M. Moore (Ed.), Handbook of distance education (pp. 129-144). Mahwah, NJ: Erlbaum.

Bernard, R. M., Abrami, P. C., Borokhovski, E., Wade, C. A., Tamin, R. M., Surkes, M. A., & Bethel, E. C. (2009). A meta-analysis of three types of interaction treatments in distance education. Review of Educational Research, 79(3), 1243-1289.

Brown, A., & Voltz, B. (2005). Elements of effective e-Learning design. The International Review of Research in Open and Distance Learning, 6(1).

Cohen, E. B. (2009). A philosophy of informing science. Informing Science: The International Journal of an Emerging Transdiscipline, 12, 1-15. Retrieved from Moore, M. G. (1989). Three types of interaction. American. Journal of Distance Education, 3(2), 1-6.

Moore, M.G. (2007). The theory of transactional distance. In M.G. Moore, Handbook of Distance Education Today, 2nd ed., Mahwah, NJ: Lawrence Erlbaum Associates.

Wagner, E. D. (1994). In support of a functional definition of interaction. The American Journal of Distance Education, 8(2), 6-26.

Wagner, E. D. (1997). Interactivity: From agents to outcomes. New Directions for Teaching and Learning, 71, 19-26.

Learning

Bandura, A. (1986). Social foundations of thought and action: A social cognitive theory. Prentice-Hall, Inc.

Bandura, A. (1977). Social learning theory. Englewood Cliffs, NJ: Prentice Hall.

Bjork, R.A. (1994). Memory and metamemory considerations in the training of human beings. In J. Metcalfe, J. & Shimamura, A. (Eds.), Metacognition: Knowing about Knowing, 185-205. Cambridge, MA: MIT Press. https://bjorklab.psych.ucla.edu/wp-content/uploads/sites/13/2016/07/RBjork_1994a.pdf

Bjork, E. L., & Bjork, R. A. (2011). Making things hard on yourself, but in a good way: Creating desirable difficulties to enhance learning. Psychology and the real world: Essays illustrating fundamental contributions to society, 56-64.

Caple, C. (1997). The effects of spaced practice and spaced review on recall and retention using computer-assisted instruction. Dissertation Abstracts International: Section B: The Sciences & Engineering, 57, 6603.

Chi, M. T. H. (2000). Self-explaining expository texts: The dual processes of generating inferences and repairing mental models. In R. Glaser (Ed.), Advances in instructional psychology (pp. 161–238). Mahwah, NJ: Lawrence Erlbaum Associates, Inc.

Chi, M. T. H., Bassok, M., Lewis, M., Reimann, P., & Glaser, R. (1989). Self-explanations: How students study and use examples in learning to solve problems. Cognitive Science, 13, 145–182.

Chi, M. T. H., DeLeeuw, N., Chiu, M.-H., & LaVancher, C. (1994). Eliciting self-explanations improves understanding. Cognitive Science, 18, 439–477.

Clark, R. (2003). Building expertise: Cognitive methods for training and performance improvement (2nd ed.). Silver Spring, MD: International Society for Performance Improvement.

Dempster, F.N. (1990). The spacing effect: A case study in the failure to apply the results of psychological research. American Psychologist, 43, 627-634.

Hattie, J. (2008). Visible Learning: A Synthesis of Over 800 Meta-Analyses Relating to Achievement, Routledge.

Lee, H.W. Lim, K.Y., Grabowski, B.L. (2008). Generative learning: Principles and implications for making meaning. In J. M. Spector, M.D. Merrill, J. van Merriënboer, & M.P. Driscoll, (Eds.) Handbook of Research on Educational Communications and Technology (3rd ed.).

Mayer, R. E. & Moreno, R. (2003). Nine ways to reduce cognitive load in multimedia learning. Educational Psychologist, 38(1), 43-52.

McDaniel, M. A., & Butler, A. C. (2011). A contextual framework for understanding when difficulties are desirable. In Successful Remembering and Successful Forgetting: A Festschrift in Honor of Robert A. Bjork (pp. 175-198). Taylor and Francis.

Merrill, M. D. (2002). First principles of instruction. Educational Technology, Research and Development, 50(3), 43–59.

Merrill, M. D. (2007). First principles of instruction: A synthesis. In R. A. Reiser & J. V. Dempsey (Eds.), Trends and issues in instructional design and technology (2nd ed., pp. 62–71). Upper Saddle River, NJ: Pearson.

Paas, F. G. W. C, & Van Merriënboer, J. J. G. (1993). The efficiency of instructional conditions: An approach to combine mental effort and performance measures. Human Factors: The Journal of the Human Factors and Ergonomics Society, 35(4): 737–743.

Roediger, H.L., III, & Karpicke, J.D. (2006). The power of testing memory: Basic research and implications for educational practice. Perspectives on Psychological Science, 1, 181-120.

Roediger, H. L., & Butler, A. C. (2011). The critical role of retrieval practice in long-term retention. Trends in Cognitive Sciences. 15 (1): 20–27.

Trowler, V. (November 2010). Student engagement literature review.

Stern, E. (2017). Individual differences in the learning potential of human beings.

Sweller, J. (2005). Implications of cognitive load theory for multimedia learning. In R. E. Mayer (Ed.), The Cambridge Handbook of Multimedia Learning (pp. 19-30). New York, NY: Cambridge University Press.

Sweller, J. (2008). Human cognitive architecture. In J. M. Spector, M. D. Merrill, J. V. Merriënboer, & M.P. Driscoll (Eds.), Handbook of Research on

Educational Communications and Technology 3rd ed., 369-381. New York, NY: Taylor & Francis Group.

Van Merriënboer, J. J. G., & Kirschner, P. A. (2001). Three worlds of instructional design: State of the art and future directions. Instructional Science, 29, 429–441.

Van Merriënboer, J. J. G., & Kirschner, P. A. (2017). Ten steps to complex learning. Routledge.

Whitten, W.B., Bjork, R.A. (1977). Learning from tests: Effects of spacing. Journal of Verbal Learning & Verbal Behavior. 16: 465–478.

Learnability

Costabile, M. F., De Marsico M., Lanzilotti R., Plantamura, V. L., & Roselli, T. (2005). On the usability evaluation of e-learning applications. Proceedings of the 38th Hawaii International Conference on System Sciences.

Grossman, T., Fitzmaurice, G., and Attar, R. (2009). A survey of software learnability: metrics, methodologies and guidelines. In Proceedings of the 27th international Conference on Human Factors in Computing Systems. New York, NY, 649-658.

Guthrie, J. T. (1972). Learnability versus readability of texts. The Journal of Educational Research, 65(6).

Memory, Cognitive Load

Ausubel, D. P. (1968). Educational Psychology: A Cognitive View. New York: Holt, Rinehart & Winston.

Chen, B., & Hirumi, A. (2009). Effects of advance organizers on learning for differentiated learners in a fully Web-based course. International Journal of Instructional Technology & Distance Learning.

Clark, R. C., Nguyen, F., & Sweller, J. (2011). Efficiency in Learning: Evidence-based Guidelines to Manage Cognitive Load. San Francisco, CA: Pfeiffer.

Metacognition

Flavell, J. H. (1979). Metacognition and cognitive monitoring: A new area of cognitive-developmental inquiry. American Psychologist, 34, 906–911.

Fogarty, R. (1994). How to Teach for Metacognition. Palatine, IL: IRI/Skylight Publishing.

Misconceptions

Chi, M. T. H. (2000). Self-explaining: The dual processes of generating inference and repairing mental models. In R. Glaser (Ed.), Advances in instructional psychology (Vol 5): Educational design and cognitive science, 161-238. Mahwah, NJ: Erlbaum.

Gooding, J. & Metz, B. (2011). From misconceptions to conceptual change. Science Teacher, 78(4), 34-37.

Nazario, G. M., Burrowes, P. A., & Rodriguez, J. (2002). Persisting misconceptions: Using pre- and post-tests to identify biological misconceptions. Journal of College Science Teaching, 31(5), 292-296.

Savion, L. (2009). Clinging to discredited beliefs: The larger cognitive story. Journal of the Scholarship of Teaching and Learning, 9, 81-92.

National Research Council. (1997). Science teaching reconsidered: A handbook. Washington, DC: The National Academies Press.

Practice

Benner, P. (1984). From novice to expert: Excellence and power in clinical nursing practice. Menlo Park: Addison-Wesley, 13-34.

Ericsson, A., & Pool, R., (2016). Peak. Secrets of the New Science of Expertise. New York: Houghton Mifflin Harcourt.

Self-direction

Duckworth, A. L., & Seligman, M. E. P. (2005). Self-discipline outdoes IQ in predicting academic performance of adolescents. Psychological Science, 16, 939-944.

Duckworth, A. L., Gendler, T. S., & Gross, J. J. (2016). Situational strategies for self-control. Perspectives on Psychological Science, 11, 35-55.

Locke, E. A. & Latham, G. P. (2002). Building a practically useful theory of goal setting and task motivation. A 35-year odyssey. American Psychologist, 57(9), 705-17.

Nilson, L. B. (2013). Creating Self-Regulated Learners: Strategies to Strengthen Students' Self-Awareness and Learning Skills. Sterling, VA: Stylus Publishing.

Oettingen, G. (2014). Rethinking positive thinking: Inside the new science of motivation. New York, NY: Penguin.

Oettingen, G. & Mayer, D. (2002). The motivating function of thinking about the future: Expectations versus fantasies. Journal of Personality and Social Psychology, 83, 1198-1212.

Oettingen, G., Pak. H., Schnetter, K. (2001). Self-regulation of goal setting: Turning free fantasies about the future into binding goals. Journal of Personality and Social Psychology, 80, 736-753.

Rana, S., Ardichvili, A., & Poesello, D. (2016). Promoting self-directed learning in a learning organization: tools and practices. European Journal of Training and Development, 40, 470-489.

Sitzmann, T. & Ely, K. (2011). A meta-analysis of self-regulated learning in work-related training and educational attainment: What we know and where we need to go. Psychological Bulletin, 137(3), 421-42.

Spacing, Retrieval practice

Benjamin, A. S., & Tullis, J. (2010). What makes distributed practice effective? Cognitive Psychology, 61, 228-247.

Dempster, F., & Farris, R. (1990). The spacing effect: Research and practice. Journal of Research and Development in Education, 23(2), 97-101.

Karpicke, J., & Blunt, J. (2011). Retrieval practice produces more learning than elaborative studying with concept mapping. Science, 331(6018). 772-775.

McNamara, D.S., Kintsch, E., Songer, N.B., & Kintsch, W. (1996). Are good texts always better? Interactions of text coherence, background knowledge, and levels of understanding in learning from text. Cognition and Instruction, 14(1), 1-43.

Roediger, H.L. & Karpicke, J.D. (2006). The power of testing memory: Basic research and implications for educational practice. Perspectives on Psychological Science, 1, 181-210.

Roediger, H.L., & Karpicke, J.D. (2006). Test-enhanced learning: Taking memory tests improves long-term retention. Psychological Science, 17, 249-255.

Reading/Readability/Writing

S. Badgley. (February 20, 2015), Should your blog reading level be about 8th grade? Lantern.

Craig, J. & Scala, I. K. (2006). Designing with Type: The Essential Guide to Typography, 5th ed. Watson-Guptill.

Federal Plain Language Guidelines (2011) www.plainlanguage.gov/howto/guidelines/FederalPLGuidelines/index.cfm

Fleming, M., & Levie, W. H. (1993). Principles from the Behavioral and Cognitive Sciences. Englewood Cliffs, NJ: Educational Technology Publications.

Hartley, J. Designing Instructional Text. (1994). London: Kogan Page Ltd.

Kellogg, R.T., Whiteford, A.P., Turner, C.E., Cahill, M., & Mertens, A. (2013) Working memory in written composition: An evaluation of the 1996 model. Journal of Writing Research, 5(2), 159-190.

Kincaid J. P., Braby, R., & Mears J. (1988). Electronic authoring and delivery of technical information. Journal of Instructional Development. 11, 8–13.

Latham, J. S. (1991). The Effect of Outlines, Headings and Summaries on the Recall of Informational Text. http://ro.ecu.edu.au/theses_hons/247

Lohr, L. (2003). Creating Graphics for Learning and Performance. Upper Saddle River, New Jersey: Pearson Education.

Mayer, R. E., Fennell, S., Farmer, L., & Campbell, J. (2004). A personalization effect in multimedia learning: Students learn better when words are in conversational style rather than formal style. Journal of Educational Psychology, 96 (2), 389-395.

Training Outcomes

Salas, E., Tannenbaum, S.I., Kraiger, K and Smith-Jentsch, K.A. (2012). The science of training and development in organizations: What matters in practice, Psychological Science in the Public Interest, 13 (2), pp. 74-101. 42.

Williams, J. & Rosenbaum, S. (2004). Learning Paths. San Francisco: Pfeiffer.

Transfer

Baldwin, T. T., & Ford, J. K. (1988). Transfer of training: A review and directions for future research. Personnel Psychology, 41, 63–105.

Burke, L.A. & Hutchins, H.M. (2007). Training transfer: An integrative literature review. Human Resource Development Review, 6, (3), 263-296.

Burke, L. and Hutchins, H. (2008). A study of best practices in training transfer and proposed model of transfer, Human Resource Development Quarterly, 19, 107–28.

Foxon, M. (1993). A process approach to the transfer of training. Australian Journal of Educational Technology, 9(2), 130-143.

Grossman, R. & Salas, E. (2011). The transfer of training: What really matters. International Journal of Training and Development, 15(2), 103-120.

Salas, E., Wilson, K. A., Priest, H. A. and Guthrie, J. W. (2006). Design, Delivery, and Evaluation of Training Systems, in Handbook of Human Factors and Ergonomics, Third Edition (ed G. Salvendy), Hoboken, NJ: John Wiley & Sons, Inc.

Usability, User Experience, Information Design

Costabile, M.F., De Marsico, M, Lanzilotti, R., Plantamura, V. L., & Roselli, T. (2005). On the usability evaluation of e-Learning applications. Proceedings of the 38th Annual Hawaii International Conference on System Sciences, 2005.

Grossman, R. & Salas, E. (2011). The transfer of training: what really matters. International Journal of Training and Development, 15(2), 102-120.

Spyridakis, J. H. (2000). Guidelines for authoring comprehensible web pages and evaluating their success. Technical Communication, 47(3), 359-282.

Usability.gov. Improving the user experience https://www.usability.gov

Usability Book of Knowledge http://www.usabilitybok.org/

World Changes

Brynjolfsson, E. & McAfee, A. (2012). Race against the machine: How the digital revolution is accelerating innovation, driving productivity, and irreversibly transforming employment and the economy. Lexington: Digital Frontier Press.

Brynjolfsson, E. & McAfee, A. (2016). The second machine age: Work, progress, and prosperity in a time of brilliant technologies. New York: WW Norton & Company.

Chui, M., Manyika, J., & Miremadi, M. (November 2015). Four fundamentals of workplace automation, McKinsey Quarterly.

Christensen, C. M. (1997). The Innovator's Dilemma: When New Technologies Cause Great Firms to Fail. Harvard Business Review Press.

Wastlund, E. (2007). Experimental Studies of Human-Computer Interaction: Working memory and mental workload in complex cognition.

Index

Baldwin, Timothy 25
Bandura, Albert 21
Behavior modeling 99
Bjork, Robert 19
Burke, Lisa 25
Chi, Michelene 118
Cognitive Load 18
   helpful and harmful 19
Connect learning objectives to job tasks 50
Deep learning 9
   and social learning 23
   differences between surface and deeper learning 10
   surface learning is not bad 10
Deming, David 21
Desirable difficulties 19
Differences between novices and experts 7
Encoding 15
Factors that affect performance 67
Feedback
   how prior knowledge affects 45
   intrinsic versus extrinsic feedback 36
   role of 44
   types that are damaging 44
Ferguson, Dave 131
Fidelity (realism) in training 90
Gawande, Atul 131
Goals
   goal setting and work performance 74
   how goals increase action 75
   team vs personal 75
   which factors impact attainment of goals 75
Grossman, Rebecca 83
Hattie, John 44
Hutchins, Holly 25
Interaction 23
   and deep learning 24
   how interaction supports learning 24
   interaction vs. interactivity 23

three types of interaction 23
Job aids 126, 131
    best times to use 127
    types 126
Job-focused training 49
Kirschner, Paul 102
Latham, Gary 74
Learnability 11
Learning objectives
Locke, Edwin 74
Marton, Ference 9
Memory 14
Metacognition 29
Misconceptions 64
Moore, Michael 23
Narciss, Susanne 44
Post-training support 107
Practice
    definition 7
    error handling 101
    for remembering 111
    for self-direction 73
    for transfer 83
    goal-oriented practice 42
    how much practice 42, 43
    match to prior knowledge 43
    more support to less support 104
    need for social interactions 96
    need for variability (range of conditions) 94
    right and wrong ways 99
    support remembering after instruction 112
    when part practice may be needed 105
    whole-skill vs part-skill 102
    why practice is critical 35
Practice and feedback
    contributuion to learning outcomes 41
    performance, objectives, practice, feedback 37
    why they go together 35
Prior knowledge 13
Readability 12
Remembering
    analyze the need for remembering 60

remembering continuum 59
remember vs automate 59
Retrieval practice ....*See* spaced remembering
Rosenbaum, Steve 41
Rosset, Allison 131
Salas, Eduardo 70, 83
Säljö, Roger 9
Schemas 13
    practice and feedback for building 13
Self-direction
    definition 73
    goals 73
    learning on one's own 74
    learning strategies 77
    role of L&D practitioners 74
Self-explanations 118
Shute, Valerie 44
Skill upkeep (maintenance) 132
    automation of 132
Social
    channels for learning 21
    learning 20
Social skills 21
Spaced learning 120
    time issues 120
    vs massed learning 120
Spaced remembering 123
    types of activities 123
Support for memory 126
Support for trained skills 70
Sweller, John 14
Tactics that influence transfer 83
Tactics to analyze the job context 50
Tactics to practice for remembering 111
Tactics to provide feedback 137
Thalheimer, Will 125
Time to proficiency 41
Transfer 25
    design and delivery variables 27
    is problematic 25
    personal characteristics 28
    role of relevancy 84

work environment influencers 26
Van Merriënboer, Jeroen J. G. 102
Whole skill practice
    simpler to more complex whole skills 103
Williams, Jim 41
Work context
    conditions 54
    environmental cues, consequences, variability, and social interactions . 89
    for remembering 112
    improves encoding 114
    realism (fidelity) 115
    social 62
    transfer 89
Working memory 15
    limits of 15

Notes

About the Author

Patti Shank is an internationally recognized learning analyst, researcher, designer, and author who is cited as a leading international learning expert. She works with organizations to analyze and find solutions for organizational performance needs and is regularly asked to speak at conferences and train trainers, instructors, designers, and experts.

Patti has authored, co-authored, or edited numerous learning books and eBooks. She was an award-winning contributing editor for *Online Learning Magazine* and the research director for the eLearning Guild. You can find her articles and research in eLearning Guild publications, Magna Publications' *Online Classroom,* eLearning Industry, and ATD's *Science of Learning* and *Senior Leaders and Executives* blogs.

Patti lives in Colorado, USA, and loves to spend time with her fur babies and friends, dance, walk, read, cook, and travel.

Made in the USA
Las Vegas, NV
26 January 2024

84931998R00118